T0300982

Human vs ChatGPT – Language of Advertising in Beauty Products Advertisements

This book systematically investigates the linguistic strategies employed in beauty product advertising to assess their persuasive and manipulative effects. The work is divided into two sections: a review of relevant literature and an empirical analysis of advertisements. The analysis initially focuses on the linguistic features of advertisements created by humans prior to the introduction of ChatGPT, examining the linguistic measures used and their methods of persuasion and manipulation. Subsequent sections provide a detailed examination of advertisements generated by ChatGPT versions 3.5 and 4.0, analysing the artificial intelligence's use of linguistic techniques. This includes a meta-analysis where ChatGPT itself discusses the linguistic strategies it employs. The ultimate goal is to compare and contrast the effectiveness and linguistic devices used in advertisements crafted by humans and those by ChatGPT, analysing how AI influences the language of advertising and its impact on consumer behaviour.

Ida Skubis, PhD, Silesian University of Technology

Dominika Kołodziejczyk, Jan Dlugosz University

Human vs ChatGPT – Language of Advertising in Beauty Products Advertisements

Ida Skubis

and Dominika Kołodziejczyk

CRC Press
Taylor & Francis Group
Boca Raton London New York

CRC Press is an imprint of the
Taylor & Francis Group, an **informa** business

First edition published 2025
by CRC Press
2385 NW Executive Center Drive, Suite 320, Boca Raton FL 33431

and by CRC Press
4 Park Square, Milton Park, Abingdon, Oxon, OX14 4RN

CRC Press is an imprint of Taylor & Francis Group, LLC

© 2025 Ida Skubis and Dominika Kołodziejczyk

ISBN: 9781032934136 (hbk)
ISBN: 9781032935621 (pbk)
ISBN: 9781003566441 (ebk)

DOI: 10.1201/9781003566441

Typeset in Times
by Deanta Global Publishing Services, Chennai, India

Contents

Introduction

Advertising is omnipresent. It is no longer merely the foundation of trade and marketing in a free-market economy but it has also entered the realm of culture. There is no chance to run away from advertising. While it may appear evident to some people how the advertisement affects us, it remains a mystery to a vast mass of others. There are some small details in advertising that make it so effective. Obviously, the prominent and ultimate power of advertising is the usage of the language and appropriate linguistic features.

Linguistic tools can be employed to impact people's views and feelings. Persuasion or manipulation deliberately influences people. The main distinction between these phenomena is that with persuasion, convincing someone to do something will not harm them later. Unfortunately, persuasion and even manipulation occur more and more often. Advertisers look for more and more sophisticated methods to mislead people and achieve personal benefits from their unawareness of being persuaded or manipulated.

The objective of this book is to present the language of advertising and analyse its persuasiveness and manipulativeness in terms of language features used in beauty products advertisements created by a human, ChatGPT 3.5, and ChatGPT 4.0.

The first chapter contains the theoretical basis, including definitions of advertising, persuasion, and manipulation. The functions of advertising, the techniques of persuasion, and the phenomena of implicature and presupposition are also discussed.

The second chapter splits linguistic features used in advertising language into three levels, appropriately the lexical, syntactical, and rhetorical levels, and examines their components.

In recent years, artificial intelligence (AI) has revolutionised numerous domains, including management, marketing, and advertising. The third chapter investigates AI's role in management and marketing, with a particular focus on its applications in advertising. The fourth chapter examines generative AI, highlighting its influence on advertising, the capabilities of ChatGPT, and the ethical issues associated with its implementation.

The fifth chapter presents a comparative analysis of advertisements for beauty products created by humans, ChatGPT 3.5, and ChatGPT 4.0. This analysis includes make-up and skin/body/hair care products, examining the differences in language and persuasiveness. Initially, advertisements created by humans are analysed based on linguistic measures used and their persuasiveness. Subsequently, both versions of ChatGPT are asked to create the advertisements, enumerate the linguistic measures used, and describe them. Afterwards, we analyse the advertisements crafted by ChatGPT 3.5 and 4.0 and evaluate them to determine if these AI models accurately recognised and used these measures.

The findings aim to demonstrate the strengths and weaknesses of human versus AI-generated advertisements in terms of linguistic features and their effectiveness. This book seeks to offer a thorough understanding of advertising language and the growing influence of AI in this domain, delivering valuable information for researchers, marketers, and AI developers.

Advertisement – The Scope of the Term

1

Advertising is an inevitable part of consumer society. It is a phenomenon that is impossible to ignore and can often provoke either delight or indignation. Recognising the core of advertising, its language, and the specificity of the advertisement text begins with a clear understanding of the notion of an advertisement and its priorities. The etymology of this word should be found in Latin sources, where the verb *advertere* means "to direct one's attention to; give heed" (Harper 2022). The word advertisement, in turn, began to be used in the early 15th century as a "written statement calling attention to (something), public notice", but the main modern sense emerged in the 1580s and was fully developed by the 18th century (Harper 2020). It can therefore be concluded that the main task of advertising is to arouse interest in a specific product.

On the one hand, the Merriam-Webster Dictionary states that an advertisement is "something (such as a short film or a written notice) that is shown or presented to the public to help sell a product or to make an announcement".[1] On the other hand, Longman Dictionary posits that an advertisement is "a icture, set of words, or a short film, which is intended to persuade people to y a product or use a service".[2] According to Dunn (in Ke and Wang 2013), a well-known American advertising expert, advertising is "any paid form of non-personal communication through various mass media by business firms, non-profit organisations, and individuals who are in some way identified in the messages and who hope to inform or persuade members of a particular audience".

In the opinion of Vanden et al. (in Richards and Curran 2002), advertising is "nonpersonal communication for products, services, or ideas that is paid for by an identified sponsor for the purpose of influencing the audience". Furthermore, the American Marketing Association states that

DOI: 10.1201/9781003566441-1

advertising is the placement of announcements and messages in time or space by business firms, nonprofit organisations, government agencies, and individuals who seek to inform and/or persuade members of a particular target market or audience regarding their goods, services, organisations or ideas.[3]

Thus, it can be simply concluded that advertising's purpose, regardless of its definition, is to inform and persuade consumers. Moreover, it is a fundamental form of communication used by a producer to reach out to potential customers and a medium for influencing consumers' feelings, beliefs, and attitudes towards a product. Hence, the capacity to develop or create messages that attract attention and foster a common understanding between the advertiser and the target audience is what provides advertising its power (in Dermawan and Barkah 2022).

1.1 MAJOR FUNCTIONS OF ADVERTISING

From creating awareness and shaping perceptions to driving consumer behaviour and supporting the economy, advertising functions are integral to the success of both products and services. By exploring these functions, we gain a deeper understanding of how advertising not only informs and persuades but also influences market dynamics and cultural trends. With the concept of advertising clarified, it is possible to proceed with its four basic and most significant functions as specified by Nowacki (2006):

1. Informational function
The primary task of the informational function is to inform the recipients of new products, including their features, prices, and conditions of sale. The market is constantly evolving and recipients cannot analyse the changes that are taking place themselves, hence the role of information provided by advertisements is notable. The most important is that the informativeness in the advertisement affects the customer's awareness of the specific product.

2. Sales promotion function
The sales promotion function is related to two types of influence on the customer: persuasion and reminder. Persuasion aims to convince the customer of the advertiser arguments and encourage them to behave in a certain way and to

buy goods in quantities convenient to the seller. Reminder, on the other hand, is mostly concerned with forming loyalty to products, brands, and places of sale.

3. Educational function
The educational function is related to the idea that marketers educate customers about new products or approaches to meeting their needs while also persuading them to use those products by emphasising the benefits that come with them.

4. Competitive function
This function is related to the broadcasting of messages in response to competitors' broadcast advertising messages. Not only does it mean advertising to increase the appeal of one's own products, but also to disrupt competitors' advertising campaigns (Nowacki 2006).

However, as claimed by Szczęsna (2001), the evolution of modern advertising is moving towards a reduction of the purely informational factor, in favour of emotional and aesthetic reception. It appears that information is becoming dominated by product praise and recipient acquisition, with persuasion or even manipulation, taking the lead.

On the one hand, the major functions of advertising are strongly associated with the *AIDA* model which was developed by American businessman St. Elmo Lewis in 1898 (Mounir, 2023). It is often referred to as the basis for successful advertising. Also, among marketing activities, the AIDA model is one of the most widely used marketing strategies (in Tristanto et al. 2021). The AIDA model is a fundamental tool for marketers, helping them to effectively design and execute complex campaigns. It outlines the four stages a customer experiences when responding to marketing communication. Wang and Ke (2013) extended this model with an additional stage (letter C), and this is how the more pertinent *AIDCA* model came about to clarify the advertisements' functions. The letters of this acronym respectively stand for:

A stands for *Attention*, and its purpose is to draw people's attention to something. When a new product is released, the purpose of advertising will be to get people to recognise it. The audience's attention can be captured in a variety of ways, depending on the medium. On the one hand, in the case of a written advertisement, it could be a non-standard shape, a unique colour, a suitable typeface, or an eye-catching drawing or photograph. In contrast, radio or television advertising may feature loud music or silence (Budzyński 2007).

I stands for *Interest*, which means to pique someone's curiosity. After capturing the customers' attention, the advertisement must maintain it and persuade them that the subject of the advertisement should be of interest to them. A catchy tagline, an engaging beginning to the advertisement's content, or a compelling turn of events in the commercial spot can all capture interest in the audience. If the advertisement captures the recipient's attention in the first few seconds of their focus, there is an excellent possibility they will watch it through to the end and be exposed to compelling arguments (ibid.).

D stands for *Desire*, and its purpose is to arouse desire. The arguments presented in the advertisement must arouse the consumer's desire to own the advertised good. The advertisement shall persuade the consumer that the product or service will fulfil a need or create a need that they have not previously felt.

C stands for *Conviction*, which means to create conviction. The buyer is persuaded that the marketed brand is greater than other competitive brands. To get action, the letter

A stands for *Action*. Directly or indirectly, the advertisement may persuade the customer to try or buy what is advertised.

This model (Wang and Ke 2013) has a huge impact on every aspect of advertising, including its structure and language.

On the other hand, according to Leech (in Vasiloaia 2018), four main functions can be distinguished:

1. Attention value

Advertisements should be written in such a way that they easily draw the attention of the target audience. This is the first requirement that determines the advertisement's effectiveness. On a linguistic level, this can be accomplished by violating linguistic standards such as incorrect spelling, neologisms, puns, solecism, rhymes, semantic deviations, and the use of words in inappropriate or unconventional circumstances.

2. Readability

The advertising style is to employ straightforward language. The recipient is always on the lookout for information that can be processed quickly and easily. Therefore, when an advertisement manages to attract the attention of the recipient, this procedure is aimed at maintaining it. Leech (in Vasiloaia 2018) came up with the term "public colloquialism" to describe a practice of using informal language related to private contexts in public or business communication. Informal styles suggest an easy-going social relationship between reader and writer, and they are characterised by informal address terms. In advertising, even the written language has many characteristics of a spoken language. First, due to a high degree of repetition and parallelism, advertising language is characterised by a high level of redundancy. Another characteristic of verbal communication that is common in advertising language is elliptic sentence forms. Furthermore, phrasal verbs, idioms, and contractions are common aspects of language of advertisement, indicating its high level of colloquialism.

3. Memorability

The message of the advertisement must be remembered by the recipient. The repetition technique is the most commonly used method for achieving this goal. From a linguistic perspective, several linguistic strategies are highly repetitive by definition and thus appear frequently in advertising language. Alliteration, metrical rhythm, rhyme, grammatical parallelism, semantic and syntactic repetitions, and lexical repeats are examples of these strategies. It is also worth mentioning that repetition and variation are frequently linked. Semantic repetition or the usage of various words from the same word field is a form of lexical variation that also works as a repetitive technique. Further to that, the frequent repeating of slogans, brands, and product names aids in the recall of the product and its associated advertising messages.

4. Selling power

Advertisements' ultimate goal is to sell. Clear directions on what to do next are the most effective way to prompt people to take the appropriate action. Imperatives are useful for stating clearly what action is important to be made and they appear frequently in advertising. Moreover, the advertisement wording attempts to be positive and uplifting to its recipients. Expressions and phrases that have a negative connotation are avoided in advertising. This method is also justifiable from a psychological and cognitive point of view since negative statements take much longer to comprehend than positive statements. The use of positive forms extend to the lexical level as well. Advertising uses euphemisms, e.g. skincare products marketed to Asian customers use the terms "lightening" or "brightening" as euphemisms for *whitening* – a term that reflects long-standing views about what is deemed beautiful. The usage of evaluative epithets with positive connotations is also prevalent. The following adjectives, according to Leech (in Vasiloaia 2018), are among the most commonly used in advertising language: new, good/better/best, sure, delicious, free, fresh, nice. All of these terms have a favourable meaning, thereby concluding that the more positivity there is, the higher the sales will be.

1.2 SEPARATING PERSUASION FROM MANIPULATION

In human communication, persuasion is a well-known and widely employed phenomenon. On a daily basis, we are exposed to persuasion via advertisements, and its effectiveness is primarily determined by the linguistic tools applied. Persuasion is the act of persuading, prompting, and encouraging through information and argumentation (Wiktor 2011). According to American expert Richard Perloff (2017), it is also "a symbolic process in which communicators try to convince other people to change their own attitudes or behaviours regarding an issue through the transmission of a message in an atmosphere of free choice" (p.649). As believed by Sokół (2008), the modern definition of persuasion should be as follows: "the flexible language should NOT say everything that the head thinks" because persuasion does not mean talking about something that is really happening but it is about consumers' expectations. To persuade means "to move by argument, entreaty, or expostulation to a belief, position, or course of action".[4] However, in the case of advertisements, it may be simplified as "the way to our YES" (Fus 2010) because the primary aim of advertisers is to create the biggest demand for a specific product.

Manipulation like persuasion falls under the area of social influence. Both are goal-oriented; the communicator's purpose is to establish or modify a particular perspective or attitude on a specific issue based on the communicator's interests. The crucial purpose of advertising is to help your target audience develop a good attitude about the product so that they become potential consumers. As specified by Wiktor (2011), the main distinguishing features of manipulation as a method of influencing another person or a social group (market segment) are as follows: hiding the goals and intentions of the subject's actions, using the other party's incomplete knowledge and unconsciousness, hiding the action itself by diverting attention from the sender of the message, deception, fragmentation of information, taking advantage of the occasions and weaknesses of someone, but also creating such occasions. According to the Merriam-Webster Dictionary, to manipulate is to "control or play upon by artful, unfair, or insidious means, especially to one's own advantage".[5]

The distinction between persuasion and manipulation begins from ethical values where in persuasive communication, there is the necessary requirement that the sender must "act in good faith" (Tokarz 2002). The moral quality of persuasion, following Harré (in Árvay 2004), is that the communicator respects their audience by considering them as humans. On the other hand, in the case of manipulation, the audience does not participate actively in the flow of communication when the speaker manipulates them; instead, the speaker regards them as objects. Although the distinction between persuasion and manipulation appears to be evident in theory, it is sometimes difficult to achieve in practice.

1.2.1 Persuasive Techniques

A persuasive technique is a sophisticated set of linguistic tools used to change attitudes and elicit responses without openly imposing ideas on the recipient. Persuasive techniques are used in advertising to build rapport and raise brand awareness rather than to increase sales (Romanowa and Smirnova 2019).

Aristotle (ibid.) refers to rhetoric, which in ancient times was the art of speaking, and indicates that the available methods of persuasion are based on three core concepts: *logos* – concerning the rational appeal, showing the speaker as a person of integrity and with a good character; *pathos* – emotional argumentation, used to excite the audience or otherwise arouse their interest; and *ethos* – moral argumentation, presenting the speaker as a trustworthy person by using cool logic and rational explanation.

Dutton (2010) identifies that there are five major axes in persuasive methods that they fit to the word *SPICE*. These are as follows:

1. Simplicity – the simpler wording, the better;
2. Perceived self-interest – convincing other people that a particular idea is good for them;
3. Incongruity – introducing solutions to confused people;
4. Confidence – being assertive;
5. Empathy – showing empathy with an aim to gain trust which increases the chance of persuading.

According to Kleppner (in Koa 2019), persuasive techniques can be classified by marketing situation and human qualities. In these terms, the scientist provides a theory of three stages of persuasion: pioneering, competitive, and retentive.

1. Pioneering stage
Kleppner (ibid.) states that the pioneering stage is used to introduce the product which has just been released. This technique intends to show that a product currently exists on the market is capable of solving a need that has previously been identified but could not be fulfilled. As a result, advertisers frequently use this technique to explain the value of the product and whether it satisfies the

requirements. This method may also be described as a means of encouraging customers to buy a new version of a product that better meets their needs than the prior one. Nowacki (2006) also claims that it is typically employed at the beginning of a product's market life cycle.

2. Competitive stage
Another technique that is used is the competitive stage. According to Kleppner (Koa 2019), the competitive stage's goal is to show or differentiate a product's stance to consumers. This indicates that advertisers inform customers about their products' market position as well as their advantages over competing products. Advertisers highlight features that make their items appear superior to similar products from competitors. They include detailed descriptions of the products, making them look more unique and different from those of other brands, in terms of both product quality and aesthetic design. Customers will believe that the product is worth buying and will provide them with satisfaction as a result. Competitive stage is used in the second and third phases of the product life cycle: growth and maturation (Nowacki 2006).

3. Retentive stage
The retentive stage is the last form of persuasion technique used in advertising. This can be regarded as an advertising reminder to clients of products that are still available in the product collection. The retentive stage is meant to guarantee that the advertised product continues to exist on the market. Most advertisers adopt this method when a product has been on the market for a long time. Retentive stage is the most important in the latter two stages of a product's life cycle: maturity and sales decrease (ibid.).

1.2.2 The Phenomenon of Implicature and Presupposition

Simple manipulative procedures can be made by using presupposition and implicature and are frequently exploited in both colloquial language contacts and public persuasion. However, in order to grasp the essence of these procedures, some definitions need to be explained. A presupposition is viewed as a relationship between sentences, or more precisely, as a relation between a surface sentence and the logical form of another (Karttunen 1974). Crystal (2008) indicates that

The philosophical uses of this term will be found in semantic discussion: a condition which must be satisfied if a particular state of affairs is to obtain, or (in relation to language) what a speaker assumes in saying a particular sentence, as opposed to what is actually asserted. It is also analysed as a certain type of logical relationship between statements, contrasting with entailment.

(p. 384)

The presupposition is a judgement that allows a sentence to be pronounced with a different judgement on the surface. Young (2017) adds that presuppositional inquiries contain notions and ideas that the listener must accept as true before considering responding. We employ this method as persuaders to convey assumptions and to lead and aid our prospects in responding to our inquiries in a way that we control and intend. We primarily want our prospects to believe what we want them to believe. We encounter a presupposition at every step. It is both functional and persuasive. It does, however, have a "flaw" – presupposition must be true or it will be accused of being false (Bralczyk 2004).

Implicature, on the other hand, does not have this "flaw". A pragmatic inference based on an utterance's conventional meaning is referred to as conventional implicature, and conversational implicatures "refer to the implications which can be deduced from the form of an utterance, on the basis of certain co-operative principles which govern the efficiency and normal acceptability of conversations" (Crystal 2008). The notion of implicature was firstly introduced by Paul Grice in 1975 in his paper "Logic and Conversation". Grice indicates the term implicature is "to account for what a speaker can imply, suggest, or mean, as distinct from what the speaker literally says" (in Fajri 2017). Fajri (2017) declares that it can be generally stated that implicatures are what speakers intend to communicate to their interlocutor beyond what is literally said and entailments of the utterance.

NOTES

1. Retrieved January 29, 2022, from https://www.merriam-webster.com/dictionary/advertisement.
2. Retrieved January 29, 2022, from https://www.ldoceonline.com/dictionary/advertisement.
3. Retrieved July 12, 2024 from https://marketing-dictionary.org/a/advertising/.
4. Retrieved January 30, 2022, from https://www.merriam-webster.com/dictionary/persuade.
5. Retrieved June 6, 2022, from https://www.merriam-webster.com/dictionary/manipulate.

Linguistic Features Used in Advertising Language

2

Language has a major impact on people and their behaviour. This is especially true in the marketing and advertising industries. The language used to convey certain messages with the goal of influencing people is crucial. Although advertising's visual content and design have a significant impact on consumers, it is the language that allows them to recognise and recall products.

The language of advertising can be categorised as a language for specific purposes (LSP). However, in order to understand the essence of advertising language as a specialised language, the definition of LSP needs to be introduced. Hoffmann (in Skubis 2020) stated that LSP is the body of linguistic means that are used in a specialist limited area of communication to ensure the agreement between people active in this area. According to Skubis (2020), while contemplating a specialised field, the subject and the activities done, i.e. the situation and the objective, are both significant and require specialised knowledge. LSP specificity, as manifested in advertising messages, consists mostly of traits such as (1) brevity, in an intentional attempt to eliminate distortions in the information provided, and (2) accuracy, to avoid both semantic and conceptual ambiguity (Díez-Arroyo 2013). Similarly, specialised language is characterised by precision, clarity, and lack of ambiguity, and most of all, specialised language consists of a specialised vocabulary (Skubis 2024). This means that a specialised language is employed to convey information concisely and precisely among professionals, and the use of specialised terminology ensures effective communication among experts in the field (Skubis 2020; Skubis et al. 2023).

DOI: 10.1201/9781003566441-2

The linguistic structure is important in the advertising message. The structure, mode of the message, and style of the advertising language all have an impact on its potential success and achievement of the stated aims. Specialists in this sector have long defined the conditions that advertising texts must fulfil in order to properly affect the recipient (Cieciura 2009). In the following, the linguistic features at three levels are introduced – appropriately lexical, syntactic, and rhetorical levels. Thanks to that division it is possible to thoroughly investigate in how many ways language influences the consumer.

2.1 LINGUISTIC FEATURES AT THE LEXICAL LEVEL

Lexis is "a term used in linguistics to refer to the vocabulary of a language, and used adjectivally in a variety of technical phrases" (p. 279) (Crystal 2008). This subsection will therefore refer to the selected lexical items that are applicable in the advertisement. Items such as monosyllabic verbs, weasel words, favourable words, personal pronouns, compounds, and neologisms will be discussed.

1. Monosyllabic verbs

Advertisers frequently use a variety of techniques to make their messages easy to understand, remember, and present in a clear and succinct manner (Linghong 2006). In their advertisements, they use simple words, particularly monosyllabic verbs. Advertisements almost always use simple monosyllabic verbs rather than the more complex multisyllabic ones. The most commonly used monosyllabic verbs in advertising, according to Fan (2013), are *buy, get, make, like, try, feel, taste, look, keep, need, see, know,* etc. In English, short words are usually the most recognisable and hence the easiest to understand. The high frequency of monosyllabic verbs in advertising also contributes to their persuasiveness.

2. Weasel words

Another strategy with a wide range of opportunities for manipulation in advertising is to make the customer believe in something about the product that is not true. Weasel word, based on Merriam-Webster Dictionary, is "a word used in order to evade or retreat from a direct or forthright statement or position".[1] Referring to Linghong (2006), while the ultimate goal of advertising is to persuade consumers to purchase a specific type of product, the word "buy" is rarely used in advertisements. This is due to the fact that the word "buy" has the connotation of "gaining something by paying money", which many people identify with their "unwilling outgoings". Accordingly, the most common weasel words are *helps virtually, acts, can be, up to, refreshes, comforts, fights, the feel of, the look of, fortified, enriched,* and *strengthened* (Danciu 2014). Advertisers employ weasel words to persuade customers that they are attempting to help them with their product rather than simply selling it.

3. Favourable words

a. Adjectives
According to the definition from the Dictionary of Stylistics (Wales 2011), an adjective is "a word class or part of speech which characteristically premodifies a noun in the so-called attributive position following the article or which occurs in the so-called predicative position, following the verb as a complement". A noun can be premodified by more than one adjective. It is a common feature in eye-catching advertisements.

The adjective, according to Anna Romanik (2014), is one of the most effective linguistic means for persuasion of values when you have a large lexical inventory at your disposal because it is the part of speech that directly indicates a feature of an object, and through it, it is easy to convey an emotional attitude towards the described object.

As Leech (in Linghong 2006) observed, "Advertising language is marked by a wealth of adjective vocabulary". Linghong (2006) states that positive adjectives, such as emotive and evaluative adjectives, are commonly applied in the set-up of advertising. Favourable adjectives reaffirm the products' attractive attributes. More significantly, they empower consumers in developing a positive attitude towards the products.

Delin (in Kaur et al. 2013), however, indicated that advertising is more than merely employing positive adjectives. In advertising, adjectives can convey both positive and negative affective meanings. The consumer's positive or negative opinion of an object given will be displayed using affective meaning. The positive adjectives are associated with the product's quality, whereas the negative adjectives are associated with difficulties that existed just before using the product or as a result of not using the product.

b. Comparative and superlative degrees
Both Teodorescu (2015) and Linghong (2006) show that advertising texts employ comparative and superlative degrees to convey the superior quality of the offered product or service. Advertisers do not make precise comparisons

between their product and others by identifying or referring to their competitors because it is illegal for them to denigrate or unfairly criticise other products or commercials. When the comparative degree is employed, there is no mention of a specific product to which the promoted product is compared, only that it is "better", "more powerful", "faster", and so on, without specifying the less competitive option (Linghong 2006). By employing superlatives, the impression is created that the marketed service or product is cutting-edge, equipped with latest technology, and the best of its kind, without disparaging others.

4. Personal pronouns
A personal pronoun is "a pronoun having a definite person or thing as an antecedent and functioning grammatically in the same way as the noun that it replaces. In English, the personal pronouns include *I, you, he, she, it, we,* and *they,* and are inflected for case".[2]

Although all advertisements are aimed at potential or existing customers, many industries choose to highlight the consumer as one of the most important parts of the advertising message. The use of *you* individualises the consumer. This direct way of addressing contributes to the impersonality of mass-media discourse. It seems to be mainstream since it implies a one-to-one connection between advertisers and recipients (Smith 2004).

According to Linghong (2006), advertising makes extensive use of the pronouns *you* and *we*. Such pronouns make the language sound more warm and friendly, assist to narrow the gap between the advertiser and the recipient, and make the advertisements more attractive. Through the use of personal pronouns, advertisers attempt to persuade the recipient that all of the products and services they offer are designed with his specific needs and benefits in mind and thus encourage the recipient to make a purchase.

Cook (in Smith 2004) also states that, in English, you can express both informal and formal relationships between the advertiser and the recipient at the same time, allowing the voice of the advertisement to simultaneously be one of friendship, authority, and respect.

5. Compounds
A Dictionary of Stylistics (Wales 2011) indicates that "by compounding, a productive means of word-formation in English, two lexical items are combined to make a new one, which is regarded as a single fixed unit, often with a meaning different from its (separate) parts".

English compounds are simple to create and come in a wide variety of forms. A compound made up of a few simple words can sometimes reveal unconventional meaning and elicit rich associations in recipients (Linghong 2006).

Rush (1998) also founds that in advertising copywriting, the possibilities for creating new and unusual compounds are limitless. For instance, beauty advertisements are well-known for their liberal use of premodifying compounds, many of which are nonce compounds, e.g. *stay-true* wear, *line-diminishing* coverage, or *age-defying* formula. Advertising compounds, unlike more traditional forms of linguistic expression, have an unusually high level of productivity. Their vivid constructions add dynamism and impact to an advertising message that must compete with a plethora of other advertising messages.

6. Neologisms

A neologism in lexicology means "a newly invented word" (Wales 2011). Neologisms are defined as newly coined lexical units or existing words that acquire new meanings (Newmark 1988). They can be created through borrowing from other languages, compounding existing words, or derivation and conversion. Thus, it can be defined that neologisms are words or word combinations which are innovative in their form or meaning.

Newmark (1988) identifies 12 types of neologisms: old words, old words with new senses, new coinages, derived words, abbreviations, collocations, eponyms, phrasal words, transferred words, acronyms, pseudo neologisms, and internationalisms. Algeo (2014) classifies the creation of new words into six types: creating, borrowing, combining, shortening, blending, and shifting, each with its subtypes (Skubis et al. 2023). For the purpose of this work, however, we concentrate on the two following examples, where neologisms can be categorised as coinages and borrowed words.

a. Coinage
In English advertisements, new words or phrases created through imitation are common. These newly coined words and phrases may imply that the advertised product has unusual qualities as well as the value of innovation. Affixes are frequently used to coin new words in English. The most commonly used include *super-*, *ex-*, *ultra-*, *auto-*, and *-aid*, e.g. *superslim* or *ultracare* (Linghong 2006).

b. Borrowed words
Since many of the products advertised are imported from other countries, advertisers may intentionally include foreign words in the advertising text to make the product appear exotic and therefore more intriguing (ibid.). Ray et al.

(1991) confirm that "the use of the foreign language is mostly for the prestige purposes".

2.2 LINGUISTIC FEATURES AT THE SYNTACTIC LEVEL

Syntax is "the study of the interrelationships between elements of sentence structure, and of the rules governing the arrangement of sentences in sequences" (Crystal 2008). Crystal (ibid.) states that studying the sequential arrangements of syntax is referred to as syntactics. In this section, sentences that appear in advertisements will be shown. These are sentences such as imperative, interrogative, short, simple, and minor.

1. Imperative and interrogative sentences
Cambridge Dictionary defines interrogative sentence as "a sentence that asks a question or makes a request for information".[3] Crystal (2008) indicates interrogative as "a term used in the grammatical classification of sentence types, and usually seen in contrast to declarative. It refers to verb forms or sentence/clause types typically used in the expression of questions". According to Wales (2011), there are two main types of interrogatives in English:

1. The so-called yes/no questions, which as their name implies, frequently expect a *yes* or *no* answer and have subject and auxiliary verb inversion;
2. The so-called *wh*-question formed through the use of interrogative pronouns and other forms (e.g. who, which, where, when, etc.).

Referring to Fan (2013), advertisers may employ interrogative sentences to create a presupposition effect, which indirectly suggests the high quality and usability of the product. The use of interrogatives proves that the advertiser is certain of the product's quality, stimulating the imagination and encouraging the consumer to buy. Linghong (2006) adds that interrogatives are primarily employed in advertising English as a rhetorical device that does not anticipate an answer or the advertisers answer the questions themselves.

Imperative sentence is "a sentence that gives a command or gives a request to do something".[4] Crystal (2008) confirms that definition with the words that "an imperative usage refers to verb forms or sentence types typically used in the expression of commands, e.g. *Go away!*". Marketing strategists repeatedly write advertisements riddled with imperatives. Imperatives are used in advertising as they seek to influence the behaviour or action of the recipient. The imperative sentences urge the recipient to take action (Torto 2016). Linghong (2006) states that imperative sentences are sometimes preferred because such sentences are persuasive and appealing to readers.

2. Short sentences

As Teodorescu (2015) notices, the length of a sentence is a significant factor in determining a text's readability. Short sentences are strongly recommendable in advertising as they raise readability. The readability of the text decreases as the sentence length increases. Moreover, it appears that nobody wants to read long advertisements. According to the research done by United Press International and the Associated Press (in Linghong 2006), a text with an average sentence length of eight words or less is considered "very easy to read", while one with an average sentence length of 29 words or more is regarded "very difficult to read", with 17 words being the ideal average.

3. Simple sentences

Apart from phrase length, sentence structure is another factor for text readability. Sentences may be simple or multiple. In the language of advertising, however, simple sentences are used more often than multiple ones. As Wales (2011) indicates, simple sentences consist of one clause only. It is preferable as it can help to reduce the difficulty of the text, convey a mood of action, and even make the text powerful (Linghong 2006).

4. Minor sentences

Some sentences in advertising texts do not follow the patterns of clause structure, nor do they follow the variations of those structures in the major syntactic classes. Minor sentences are contained in such. Merriam-Webster Dictionary defines a minor sentence as "a word, phrase, or clause functioning as a sentence and having in speech an intonation characteristic of a sentence but lacking the grammatical completeness and independence of a full sentence".[5]

According to Crystal (2008), *minor* is "a term used by some linguists in the classification of sentence types to refer to a sentence (a minor sentence) with limited productivity (e.g. Please, Sorry) or one which lacks some of the constituents of the language's major (or favourite) sentence type (e.g. vocatives, elliptical constructions)".

Wales (2011) notices that these are frequently used in magazine and bill-board advertising to convey informality, e.g. *L'Oreal. Because you're worth it.* Linghong (2006) states that those kind of sentences sound brisk and rhythmic. They are also visually appealing, so in that case advertising messages are more clearly presented and easily memorised.

2.3 LINGUISTIC FEATURES AT THE RHETORICAL LEVEL

Rhetoric in English derives from the Greek adjective *rhêtorikê* with the first recorded usage of this phrase found in Plato's *Gorgias.*[6] Plato itself perceived rhetoric as "the art of enchanting the soul".[7] Rhetoric, as defined by Crystal (2008), concerns "the way words could be arranged in order to achieve special stylistic effects". This arrangement focuses on employing language to captivate, convince, and impact an audience rather than just the structure of sentences. Barnali (2015) posits that rhetorical items are used to enhance the beauty, variety, vividness, force, and power of language. Items such as metaphor, personification, simile, alliteration, hyperbole, euphemism, parallelism, and punning serve to enhance communication, making it more engaging and touching. These items are thoroughly examined in this chapter, emphasising on how language uses them to create stylistic effects and express complex meanings. Understanding its applications and effects helps discover how language can be skilfully used to accomplish particular communication objectives.

1. Metaphor

The word *metaphor* comes from the Greek word *metaphora*, which means "a transfer", especially of the sense of one word to a different word, literally "a carrying over" (Harper 2022).

As Merriam-Webster Dictionary states, a metaphor is "a figure of speech in which a word or phrase literally denoting one kind of object or idea is used in place of another to suggest a likeness or analogy between them (as in drowning in money)".[8] Collins Dictionary declares that a metaphor can be also a symbol or an emblem.[9] Wales (2011) claims that it is a common rhetorical figure or trope. The seminal work of Lakoff and Johnson's *Metaphors We Live By* from 1980 was revolutionary by highlighting the significance of metaphor to human cognition. According to authors, it is a commonly held belief that humans are able to see, comprehend, and feel abstract ideas, e.g. *time, love,* and *argument* in terms of concrete phenomena, e.g. *money, journey*, and *war*, respectively (in Pérez-Sobrino 2013). When words are used metaphorically, one field or domain of reference is carried over or mapped onto another based on some perceived similarity between the two. Kövecses (2010) observes that majority of the specific source domains seem to characterise not just one target concept but several. For instance, the concept of *war* applies not only to *argument* but also to *love*.

Metaphors are a common way for copywriters to communicate a point to the consumer in advertising. Today, marketers use metaphors, either verbally or visually with pictures. It is essential in the advertising industry to be precise with any statement so that a message is not misinterpreted. As a result, when there are metaphors in advertising, copywriters frequently tread creatively around the truth. One method is to use phrases with only nouns rather than full sentences. The use of metaphors in advertising is likely to elicit some type of emotion from a customer and make the message memorable, which is the key to a successful advertising campaign (Barnali 2015).

2. Personification

Personification is "a figure of speech or trope in which an inanimate object, animate nonhuman, or abstract quality is given human attributes: a kind of metaphor" (Wales, 2011). By endowing non-human elements with human qualities, advertisers can make their advertising messages more engaging and relatable. It enables consumers to visualise and emotionally connect with abstract concepts or inanimate objects. Personification can highlight specific characteristics or themes, making them more memorable.

Analysing cosmetics advertisements, Maćkiewicz (in Lewiński 1999) concludes that the image of the world in advertising consists of three metaphors that are personifications: the environment is the enemy, the skin is the woman, and the cosmetics are the defender. A skin that a powerful and dangerous attacker has attacked requires a defender. This defender and friend are merely cosmetics. And, if the opponent is considered to be dangerous and his attack is ongoing, the beauty products must be seen as a necessary defender and used constantly. Barnali (2015) adds that the personification in English advertising appears to give emotion and life to products. Furthermore, it fosters more trust and affection in potential customers, arousing a greater desire for the purchase.

3. Simile

According to the definition from the Merriam-Webster Dictionary, a simile is "a figure of speech comparing two unlike things".[10] Chuandao[11] adds that similes should have at least one quality or characteristic in common. Barnali (2015) indicates that a simile compares two things explicitly by the use of a connective, typically *like, as, than*, or a verb like *resembles*. Sloane (2006) summarises these informations into a single definition:

> Simile expresses a relationship of likeness and is indicated by the linguistic markers *as* or *like*; it involves a comparison between two objects or concepts that are connected through a shared quality, the *tertium comparationis*, in contrast to the metaphor, which is often defined as a simile in an elliptic form, the simile denotes a relationship of likeness *expressis verbis*.

> *(p. 716)*

Since Aristotle's *Rhetoric*, simile has frequently been set side by side with metaphor, which involves the juxtaposition of two frames of reference. However, metaphor is far more dynamic than a simile. Referring to philosopher Donald Davidson, similes are (trivially) true but most metaphors are (patently) false (Wales 2011).

4. Alliteration

According to Vasiloaia (2018), alliteration can be defined as "literary technique, in which successive words (more strictly, stressed syllables) begin with the same consonant sound or letter". Wales (2011) states that it is the "repetition of the initial consonant in two or more words". Similarly, Sloane (2006) notes that alliteration is "an isophoneme that repeats an identical consonant at the beginning of successive words, thus creating a flow of similar sound structure" (p. 569). Ruban and Backiavathy (in Shariq 2020) suggest that alliteration adds a musical quality and enhances the appeal and engagement of reading. Alliteration may be an artistic constraint that the narrator uses to sway the audience to feel some type of emotional effect. *H* and *L* sounds, for example, can be soothing, whereas *P* or *B* sounds can be percussive and attention-grabbing. *S* sounds can imply danger or lead the audience to believe they are being tricked.[12] Chuandao[13] also notices that advertising words can be made more rhythmic and pleasing by using alliteration. Due to their common characteristic of being strongly stressed or accented, the alliterated syllables and the rhythmic pattern are related (Wales 2011). Sloane (2006) believes that slogans tend to employ alliteration to highlight advertising messages and make them memorable. People usually fall in love with the advertisement at first sight because of the figure of speech. Alliteration is used in advertisements to enhance the effects of the advertising words and the general appeal of the advertisement.

5. Hyperbole

The etymology of hyperbole should be found in Greek sources, where the verb *hyperbole* means "exaggeration, extravagance" and literally "a throwing beyond" (Harper 2022). George Puttenham, in his work *The Arte of English Poesie* from 1589 (in Wales 2011), called it the "over-reacher". Barnali (2015) posits that hyperbole, as a figure of speech, is a deliberate overstatement or extravagant exaggeration of fact used to produce a serious or comic effect. Sloane (2006) adds that hyperbole exceeds the truth and reality of things. Exaggerated statements, or rather overstatements, are used in advertising to highlight specific features of products or services. By making false promises about a product, hyperbole is also a king of association. Wales (2011) states that this figure of speech is "often used for emphasis as a sign of great emotion or passion". Hyperbole also frequently appears in common usage as an exaggerated part of a nominal compound, a comparative, a superlative, an upgrading adjective, or a numerical overstatement (Sloane 2006). Aaccording to Thorson and Duffy, it is a type of puffery that involves the use of "harmless superlatives". According to the authors, the primary purpose of puffery is to appeal to consumers' emotions rather than reason (Prelipceanu 2013).

6. Euphemism

Euphemism, derived from the Greek meaning *well-speak* (Dalamu 2018), was first attested in English in 1793 with the sense of 'choosing a less distasteful word or phrase than the one meant' (Harper 2022). Lexico Dictionary defines a euphemism as "a mild or indirect word or expression substituted for one considered to be too harsh or blunt when referring to something unpleasant or embarrassing".[14] Rasakumaran (2018) indicates that to be deemed a euphemistic, a term must be analysed in context, the effect it intends to produce with its use, and the intents of the speakers. From a synchronic standpoint, a word may only be deemed euphemistic if its meaning is hard to ascertain, allowing for two interpretations of the event, one literal and the other euphemistic. When it comes to advertisements, euphemism is more consciously used to mitigate uncomfortable issues to present a more positive or brighter image. In the language of advertising, for instance, fat old women do not exist, only fuller, mature figures (Wales 2011). Szczęsna (2001) gives more examples, e.g. stench – unpleasant smell, dirt – germs. The scientist also states that if finding a euphemism is difficult, negative connotations are placed in the context of affirmative terms that neutralise unpleasant feelings. As explained by Wales (2011), euphemism can set up a false "rose-coloured" world view and serve as a way of legitimisation.

7. Parallelism

Parallelism has been known since ancient times, under the Greek terms *parison* and *parisōsis*. Their application relates to the general artifice through which discourse is segmented into equivalent and thus comparable members (Sloane 2006). It is a rhetorical device that relies on the concept of equivalence, as defined by Roman Jakobson (in Wales 2011), or on the repeating of the same structural pattern: most typically between phrases or clauses. As determined by Chuandao,[15] parallelism stands for "the parallel presentation of two or more than two similar or relevant ideas in similar structural forms". A parallelism is an approach that is highly beneficial in advertising due to the fact that the main purpose of advertisements is to persuade and manipulate the consumer, which can be easily achieved when a slogan is repeated and so memorised by the consumer. It also functions as a means of cohesion by ensuring coherence in the advertising texts (Barnali 2015).

8. Punning

The word *pun* is not very old. Based on the Oxford Dictionary of English Etymology (in Culler 2005), it seems to have emerged shortly after 1660 and is of undetermined origin. Puns may have originated as an abbreviation for the Italian *puntiglio*, which means "small or fine point". Wales (2011) states that a pun is formed by using a polysemous term to indicate two or more meanings, or by using homonyms, which are various words that look or sound the same but have different meanings. Culler (2005) propose more expanded definition as it follows: the pun is "a figure in which, by means of a modification of sound, or change of letters, a close resemblance to a given verb or noun is produced, so that similar words express dissimilar things". Puns are often used to create humour, emphasise a point, or convey multiple layers of meaning in a single phrase. Simplified and humorous statements are easier to remember, which can help in reinforcing the advertising message. According to Barnali (2015), a pun is one of the most widely used forms of wordplay and one of the most common and efficient figures of speech in advertising. Puns can be applied in three ways:

1. By employing an ambiguous word.
2. By employing the same word in many contexts.
3. By employing terms that sound similar but have different meanings.

Chuandao[16] notices that a pun makes words implicit, amusing, and noticeable and can trigger people's associations, leaving a lasting effect on consumers.

NOTES

1. Retrieved June 6, 2022, from https://www.merriam-webster.com/dictionary/ weasel%20word.
2. Retrieved May 4, 2022, from https://www.collinsdictionary.com/dictionary/english/personal-pronoun.
3. Retrieved May 4, 2022, from https://dictionary.cambridge.org/dictionary/english /interrogative-sentence.
4. Retrieved May 4, 2022, from https://dictionary.cambridge.org/dictionary/english /imperative-sentence.
5. Retrieved May 5, 2022, from https://www.merriam-webster.com/dictionary/ minor%20sentence.
6. Retrieved July 8, 2024, from https://capone.mtsu.edu/jcomas/rhetoric/etymology .html.
7. Retrieved July 8, 2024, from https://www.americanrhetoric.com/rhetoricdefinitions.htm.
8. Retrieved May 28, 2022, from https://www.merriam-webster.com/dictionary/ metaphor.
9. Retrieved July 8, 2024, from https://www.collinsdictionary.com/dictionary/english/metaphor.
10. Retrieved June 7, 2022, from https://www.merriam-webster.com/dictionary/ simile#note-1.
11. Retrieved May 28, 2022, from http://languageinindia.com/march2005/adverti singenglishhongkong2.html.
12. Retrieved October 15, 2024, from https://www.oxfordreference.com/display/10 .1093/acref/9780198609810.001.0001/acref-9780198609810-e-2504
13. Retrieved May 28, 2022, from http://languageinindia.com/march2005/adverti singenglishhongkong2.html.
14. Retrieved June 7, 2022, from https://www.lexico.com/definition/euphemism.
15. Retrieved May 28, 2022, from http://languageinindia.com/march2005/adverti singenglishhongkong2.html.
16. Retrieved May 28, 2022, from http://languageinindia.com/march2005/adverti singenglishhongkong2.html.

AI in Management

3

Artificial intelligence (AI), a multidisciplinary field, includes virtual reality, neural networks, expert systems, and more (Haenlein and Kaplan 2021; Taherdoost and Madanchian 2023). It increases productivity and creativity at all organisational levels, helping businesses achieve their objectives and improve profitability by becoming more competitive, decreasing expenses, tightening security, and ensuring continuous data flow (Yano 2017).

AI changes the management processes, introducing advanced technologies such as AI-driven decision-making tools, autonomous robots, or even humanoid robots into the workplace which reflect a strategic emphasis on enhancing performance through human-machine collaboration. This fusion of technology and human management is meant to enhance efficiency, streamline operations, and foster innovative business practices.

While historically underexplored in management control research, AI's implications are now increasingly recognised, especially given its limited use in practice until recently (Appelbaum et al. 2017; Elbashir et al. 2011). This represents a fundamental change in how information is processed and understood in organisations, moving from predefined principles to learning-based approaches that adapt and refine predictive models (Sundström 2024; Schildt 2017).

The transition to AI analytics invokes new tensions within existing management control systems, as these systems must now integrate more dynamic, data-driven methods (Fourcade and Healy 2016). This integration often reveals an epistemological tension between the new inductive methods and the traditional deductive practices, leading to potential changes in management roles and practices (Lambert and Sponem 2012; Morales and Lambert 2013; Sundström 2024). Moreover, as AI technologies like machine learning (ML) begin to redefine performance metrics and management theories, they pose challenges to the relevance and function of traditional accounting practices, potentially leading to what some scholars describe as a crisis of "relevance lost" in the field (Johnson and Kaplan 1987; March 1987).

Furthermore, the broader adoption of AI and LLP is reshaping the management practices. The introduction of technologies such as ChatGPT has shifted the focus from simple automated tasks to complex analytical processes that assist in decision-making and strategic management (Quattrone 2016; Fleming 2019). This change not only affects the roles of accountants and managers but also prompts a re-evaluation of how management control systems are designed and implemented.

On the infrastructural level, there is a move towards more flexible, data-centric systems known as "data lakes", which contrast sharply with the structured, purpose-built databases traditionally used in management control (Kornberger et al. 2017). These changes necessitate a rethinking of how information infrastructures are designed to accommodate the fluid nature of data and decision-making processes in contemporary organisations (Sundström 2024).

Fridgeirsson et al. (2021) discuss the application and impact of AI in project management and its broader implications in the labour market. AI is described as a system that interprets external data to perform specific tasks, with a knowledge base that accumulates as the machine learns (Kaplan and Haenlein 2019). The use of AI in project management is not entirely new and involves analysing large datasets to identify patterns and trends, automate tasks, and make real-time adjustments to projects (Foster 1988; Munir 2019). AI methods are particularly well-suited for rule-based project management schedules, including those that are constrained by resources, time, cost, and risk (Foster 1988). AI can also accelerate and enhance the process of building project networks, enabling automatic completion of management tasks. Furthermore, AI can guide the direction of a project and assist in decision-making processes (Munir 2019).

AI's implementation also prompts a re-evaluation of management roles, particularly in light of its impact on employment. Frey and Osborne noted that 47% of jobs in the USA are at high risk of automation (Frey and Osborne 2017). Another study highlighted that around 14% of jobs in OECD countries could become highly automated, affecting job occupations significantly (in Fridgeirsson et al. 2021).

AI is expected to transform project management by automating tasks and enhancing decision-making through predictive analytics (Lahmann 2018). However, the implementation of AI in project management faces challenges such as lack of understanding, the cost of implementation, and the need for large standardised datasets (Lahmann 2018; Fridgeirsson et al. 2021).

Despite the potential of AI, there remains a need for human project managers, especially for tasks requiring empathy, emotional intelligence, and decision-making. It is underlined by various researchers that AI can assist project managers by providing data-driven information and freeing up time for more complex tasks, thereby enhancing productivity and value delivery (Munir 2019; Somasundaram et al. 2020; Skubis and Wodarski 2023).

The discussion around the impact of novel technologies, particularly artificial intelligence, on management roles suggests a nuanced effect. According to Frey and Osborne (2013), while many workers face high risks of automation, managers are less likely because their roles require social intelligence. Pulliainen (in Noponen 2019) echoes this sentiment, noting that senior managers view AI as a tool to enhance efficiency rather than a replacement threat. Supporting this perspective, Jarrahi (2018) emphasises AI's potential to augment the intuitive decision-making of human managers, and Autor (2015) highlights that technology historically augments human skills rather than merely replacing labour, also creating new tasks and boosting productivity.

The collaboration between humans and AI in management involves combining distinct strengths of both to enhance business performance significantly. Skubis and Wodarski (2023) emphasise the integration of human creativity, leadership, and social skills with the speed, scalability, and analytical capabilities of AI. To maximise the benefits of this partnership, Wilson and Daugherty (2018) suggest a framework based on five principles: reimagining business processes, encouraging experimentation, guiding AI strategy, responsible data management, and redesigning work to develop relevant skills.

Haesevoets et al. (2021) further illustrate that many managers are open to this collaborative approach, provided that there is a substantial human role in critical decision-making areas. Raisch and Krakowski (2020) explore the strategic options of automation versus augmentation, with the former minimising human input for efficiency and the latter enhancing human capabilities with AI support. This choice significantly affects the implementation of AI in roles that range from routine to complex decision-making scenarios.

The limitations of AI in management are noteworthy. Braga and Logan (2017) as well as Raisch and Krakowski (2020) point out that AI lacks self-awareness, intuition, and emotions, which are crucial for leadership roles involving ethical judgements and interpersonal interactions. Therefore, while AI can perform predefined tasks effectively, it cannot replace humans in functions that require emotional intelligence, such as HR management and complex problem-solving.

The article by Gümüsay et al. (2022) discusses the role of artificial intelligence in management decision-making processes. AI is defined as a computational tool capable of learning and solving complex problems traditionally requiring human intelligence. The use of AI enables businesses to implement new, data-driven decision-making methods that are automated, augmented, and altered. This technological advancement is significant for managers responsible for key organisational decisions. AI's influence is growing in various sectors, including criminal sentencing, hiring, and financial services, where it assists in both routine and critical decisions.

The authors (ibid.) highlight three primary types of decisions in management: structured, semi-structured, and unstructured, each differing in their suitability for AI assistance.

Structured decisions, which are tactical and frequent, benefit most from AI due to their reliance on large datasets and the need for quick processing. Examples include pricing and digital advertising, where AI can automate processes effectively.

Semi-structured decisions, which occur less frequently and require diverse information, are less amenable to full automation but can still benefit from AI through expert systems that provide recommendations rather than decisions. This is seen in areas like anti-money laundering programmes in banks.

Unstructured decisions involve strategic thinking about unique situations, such as mergers or product development, where AI supports decision-making by providing data analysis rather than making decisions itself. This includes using AI for analysing market trends or assessing changes via satellite imagery.

Arntz, Gregory, and Zierahn (2016) argue that not all tasks within a job are likely to be automated soon, suggesting a task-based analysis is more appropriate for predicting the impact of AI on jobs. Sintonen and Auvinen (2009) discuss the concept of leadership in the context of digital and AI-driven management, highlighting that leadership power becomes ambiguous when integrated with digital platforms. They argue that in such settings, it is the narrative or the story embedded in the organisation that leads, rather than any individual leader. Such a change raises questions about who is truly in control, especially when algorithmic management allows for precise commands but lacks transparency in decision-making processes. Despite these challenges, Noponen (2019) acknowledge the significant benefits of AI and technological advancements in enhancing quality of life and productivity, underlying the importance of equitable distribution of the benefits.

The article by Gümüsay et al. (2022) also points out the challenges and implications of AI integration in management, questioning how AI will coexist with human managers without diminishing the value of human judgement. It suggests a future where AI not only aids but also potentially governs decision-making processes, necessitating a re-evaluation of the roles and methods of human managers in an AI-driven environment. It encourages a broader reflection on how decision-making will evolve with the increasing integration of AI into managerial functions. According to Gümüsay et al. (2022), there are three types of decisions in terms of AI:

1. Earlier decision-making

As indicated by the scientists (ibid.), AI can now perform cognitive tasks previously done by humans, particularly using predictive machine learning models. This allows managers to make decisions earlier and more efficiently. For example, AI can analyse data for product introductions, determining the best market entry strategies more swiftly and in greater detail than human managers. While AI handles tactical decisions, managers can focus on broader strategies. However, AI's probabilistic nature can lead to incorrect predictions, requiring careful planning and precautions from managers.

2. Simulated decision-making

AI helps managers by simulating various future scenarios, helping in better planning. AI can automatically activate strategies under certain conditions, optimising operations in advance. For instance, Amazon uses AI to simulate scenarios affecting its operations, allowing managers to plan effectively. Future advancements will enable proactive decisions about hypothetical situations, freeing managers to focus on long-term strategies while AI handles immediate reactions.

3. Complementary decision-making

And finally, AI is expected to augment rather than replace human strategic decision-making. AI provides input, but humans make the final decisions, such as in medical diagnoses or predicting criminal behaviour. AI can reflect human biases, raising concerns about accountability and responsibility. The relationship between humans and AI in decision-making requires careful consideration, especially regarding who is accountable and has authority.

Overall, AI enhances decision-making by enabling earlier, simulated, and complementary decisions, but managers must adapt their approaches and remain vigilant about biases and accountability.

In terms of decision-making and enormous changes made by AI and robots in management, there is another aspect that evokes many controversies that may change the corporate management and generally the management processes, it is namely the introduction of humanoid robots into managerial roles which is transforming traditional management structures. These robots blend advanced data processing with decision-making capabilities. Studies by Yam et al. (2022) and by Gombolay et al. (2015) have demonstrated that robots can excel in tasks like team coordination and task allocation, often surpassing human performance. Despite this, the emotional and intuitive aspects of human interaction remain irreplaceable in certain contexts, necessitating a balanced approach to human-robot collaboration in the workplace.

The deployment of humanoid robots as CEOs, such as the examples of Mika and Tang Yu, highlights the developing role of AI in executive management. Mika, a humanoid robot, serves as the CEO of a luxury rum producer and, as stated on the company's website and in interviews with the company's owner, she plays a key role in corporate communication and decision-making, aligning with strategic goals without human biases. On the other hand, Tang Yu, a virtual humanoid robot, focuses on optimising operational efficiencies and logical decision-making within a video game company. Both cases underline the importance of human oversight to ensure that these AI entities align with organisational values and adapt to dynamic business environments, addressing ethical considerations and unexpected challenges (Skubis and Wodarski 2023).

The digitalisation of most tasks and the appearance of digital documents and knowledge management (KM) systems revolutionised information administration in the 20th century (Salloum et al. 2018; Taherdoost and Madanchian 2023). In the 21st century, KM is essential for businesses, enhancing their economic value and recognising the importance of knowledge and information globally (Cooke and Leydesdorff 2006).

KM is a method for organising specialised knowledge for efficient retrieval and re-use, involving both internal and external management to provide value to companies (Lee et al. 2007; Liebowitz 2000). Combining principles from IT, organisational behaviour, and HR management, KM fosters institutional learning, growth, innovation, and success (Lee et al. 2007). AI has become crucial for KM, advancing information acquisition, development, and application within businesses (Alhashmi et al. 2019; Salloum et al. 2018).

Recent studies explore advancements in KM systems, methods, and best practices, emphasising AI's role in these areas. AI technologies, including deep learning and neural networks, enhance KM by replicating human intelligence and providing accurate predictions (Brynjolfsson and Mitchell 2017). The relationship between AI and KM needs to be explored to harness AI effectively for a data-driven future. Organisations must adapt to new divisions of work between humans and intelligent machines, requiring new skills and competencies (Liebowitz 2000; Wu and Hu 2018; Sanzogni et al. 2017).

AI and KM are indispensable commercial tools, with AI and blockchain restructuring information management within enterprises (Chen and Liu 2018; Taherdoost 2023; Qi and Zhu 2021). Centralised big-data-processing platforms enable AI applications to manage large data volumes, offering customised knowledge patterns (van Zelst et al. 2018).

KM has been a critical field for over 30 years, explaining how information is produced, developed, maintained, and used within organisations or nations (Taherdoost and Madanchian 2023). It provides a competitive advantage for organisational success, benefiting both employees and organisations

(Nickerson and Zenger 2004). AI enhances KM by offering solutions at each stage of the KM process, enabling stakeholders to take appropriate actions more efficiently (Alani et al. 2019).

3.1 AI IN MARKETING

Artificial intelligence has significantly transformed the branch of marketing, promising profound changes through automation and personalisation, and becoming a key element in developing innovative strategies and practices in a rapidly digitising world. AI's journey in marketing began with its applications in data analytics and ML, focusing initially on streamlining large datasets and predicting consumer behaviour through basic patterns (Ma and Sun 2020; Yeği̇n 2020).

It is essential to underline that customer experience is highly valued as a key success factor among service providers at strategic, tactical, and operational levels. Effective communication is a critical aspect of advertising. Marketing behaviour has changed from traditional methods to digital interactions, where engaging customers effectively is crucial for creating memorable service experiences (Skubis and Akahome 2022; Skubis and Damas 2024).

From 2017 onwards, significant attempts have been made to classify ML and AI applications in marketing. Notably, Davenport and Ronanki (2018), in collaboration with Deloitte, categorised AI applications into three types: robotics and cognitive automation, cognitive insights, and cognitive engagement. These categories encompass automating back-office tasks, discovering data patterns, and engaging consumers through chatbots and intelligent agents (De Mauro et al. 2022).

Other classifications of AI and ML applications in marketing are often based on marketing strategies like segmentation, targeting, and positioning (STP) and on the four marketing actions or the 4Ps: product, price, place, and promotion. Corbo et al. (2022) highlighted that AI can enhance personalised advertisements and data mining, which helps in defining market segments by uncovering patterns that may not be evident through human analysis. Jarek and Mazurek (2019) illustrated how AI applications reflect the marketing mix, with examples like hyper-personalisation in products, automated payment systems for pricing, and the use of IoT for optimising retail processes.

Today, these applications have expanded exponentially due to advancements in computational power and AI technologies, allowing marketers to undertake complex predictive analytics and personalise interactions at an individual level (Şenyapar 2024; Vlačić et al. 2021).

AI presence in marketing, starting from its early adoption in data analytics and machine learning, has revolutionised how businesses engage with and understand their customers. It facilitates the processing of vast amounts of data, enabling predictive analytics to forecast consumer behaviour and personalise marketing efforts tailored to individual preferences (Yau et al. 2021; Huang and Rust 2022; Ma and Sun 2020; Yeğin, 2020; Vlačić et al. 2021).

This technology can distinguish faces and objects, enabling more targeted business applications such as security and personalised marketing based on customer preferences. AI not only enhances user engagement and lead conversion through tools like AI chatbots and smart email marketing but also optimises content delivery by analysing vast data sources, including social media and online reviews (Haleem et al. 2022; Verma 2021, Dimitrieska et al. 2018; Yang et al. 2021).

In digital marketing, AI's role extends to refining client interactions on platforms like Facebook and Instagram, where it personalises advertisements based on detailed user data. It also aids marketers in anticipating trends, optimising expenditures, and ensuring effective ad spending. Additionally, AI capabilities in recognising images contribute to diverse fields, including public security and medical imaging, hinting at its expansive future potential (Forrest and Hoanca 2015; Dumitriu and Popescu 2020).

Digital platforms provide innovative methods to influence consumer decisions and behaviours. Companies now prioritise understanding consumer preferences and behaviours through digital analytics, allowing them to tailor their marketing and advertising strategies more effectively (Skubis and Mosek 2024). By analysing data points such as browsing history, purchase records, and social media activity, AI enables the creation of highly personalised content. This targeted approach not only enhances the customer experience but also significantly improves engagement rates, fostering deeper brand loyalty (Şenyapar 2024; Ameen et al. 2021; Daqar and Smoudy 2019; Mathew and Scholar 2021). Tools like AI-driven chatbots and virtual assistants contribute further by offering 24/7 customer service, providing timely responses and gathering insights into customer preferences (Wołk et al. 2022; Chen et al. 2021; Lee 2020).

AI excels in predictive analytics, using advanced ML models to forecast market trends and consumer behaviour. This predictive capacity allows businesses to be proactive, crafting marketing strategies that align with anticipated changes in the marketplace. By identifying potential growth areas or shifts in consumer preferences before they manifest broadly, companies can allocate resources more effectively and gain a competitive edge (Mokhtari et al. 2021; Ray et al. 2018).

Beyond personalisation and predictive analytics, AI significantly enhances operational efficiency in marketing. Automated systems take over repetitive tasks such as customer segmentation, campaign analysis, and even content creation, freeing human marketers to focus on strategic and creative endeavours. This not only boosts productivity but also improves the creative quality of marketing outputs (Raiter 2021; Wang 2022).

Various sectors are using AI to support their marketing strategies. For example, Amazon Prime Air is using drones to automate its shipping and delivery processes, aiming to enhance efficiency and customer satisfaction. Similarly, Domino's Pizza is experimenting with autonomous vehicles and delivery robots to bring pizza directly to customers' doors, adding convenience and novelty to the delivery experience. Additionally, RedBalloon is employing an AI marketing platform called Albert to discover and reach new customer segments. Macy's On Call uses natural language processing to provide real-time personal assistance to shoppers in-store, thereby improving customer service. Lexus has collaborated with IBM Watson to create TV commercial scripts, demonstrating AI's capability in generating creative content. Affectiva is using affective analytics to measure consumers' emotions while watching commercials, aiming to fine-tune marketing strategies based on emotional responses. Furthermore, Replika, a machine learning-based chatbot, offers emotional support to consumers by adapting to their communication styles, illustrating AI's potential in personalised customer interactions (Huang and Rust 2021).

AI supports promotion actions through social media marketing, mobile marketing, and search engine optimisation, automating tasks such as media planning and real-time bidding. Huang and Rust (2021) distinguish three types of AI:

1. Mechanical AI is best for standardisation. Its consistent nature is used in marketing through collaborative robots (cobots) for packaging, drones for distributing goods, self-service robots for service delivery, and service robots for automating social presence on the frontline. These applications aim to deliver standardised, reliable outcomes.
2. Thinking AI excels in personalisation by recognising patterns in data, such as text mining, speech recognition, and facial recognition. This is particularly useful for personalised recommendation systems, like Netflix's movie recommendations and Amazon's cross-selling recommendations.
3. Feeling AI offers rationalisation benefits by recognising and responding to emotions, making it ideal for customer service and other marketing functions involving customer interaction. It enhances areas like customer satisfaction, handling complaints, and addressing emotions in advertising.

Davenport et al. (2020) proposed a framework to help in understanding and anticipating the future impact of AI on marketing and business. This framework includes three AI-related dimensions:

1. Level of intelligence: this dimension distinguishes between task automation and context awareness.
2. Task type: this differentiates between the analysis of numeric data (e.g. numbers) and non-numeric data (e.g. text, voice, images, facial expressions).
3. Robot embedding: this considers whether the AI is embedded in a physical robot, situated along the virtuality–reality continuum.

Similarly, Kaplan and Haenlein (2019) classified AI applications based on the level of intelligence into three categories:

1. Analytical AI: exhibits cognitive intelligence.
2. Human-inspired AI: exhibits both cognitive and emotional intelligence.
3. Humanised AI: exhibits cognitive, emotional, and social intelligence.

Both frameworks by Davenport et al. (2020) and by Kaplan and Haenlein (2019) emphasise the level of intelligence as a key classification criterion, which presents significant opportunities for enhancing customer orientation and interaction. However, these opportunities also come with challenges, particularly in maximising the effective use of AI while addressing potential difficulties in implementation.

There is also a term of "hybrid intelligence". Hybrid intelligence, also known as human–AI collaboration, combines the strengths of both human intelligence and artificial intelligence to achieve better outcomes than either could achieve alone (Andonians 2023; Huang and Rust 2022). This concept is particularly impactful in marketing, where the combination of AI and human capabilities can lead to enhanced customer experiences and improved campaign management, especially with the advancements in generative AI (Davenport and Mittal 2023).

In marketing, hybrid intelligence can significantly enhance customer experience and personalisation. AI excels at analysing vast amounts of customer data, identifying preferences, and predicting behaviour patterns as it was mentioned before. These aspects enable marketers to tailor content, offers, and interactions to individual customers. However, human judgement and creativity are crucial in using these insights to create engaging and relevant marketing materials. This combination results in a more adjusted, personalised and effective marketing strategy, as humans can intuitively understand and respond to the emotional and contextual nuances of customer interactions (Petrescu and Krishen 2023; Verhoef et al. 2015).

Another major benefit of hybrid intelligence in marketing is the optimisation of campaign management and analytics. AI can automate routine tasks, optimise decisions, and provide valuable information from data analysis. Meanwhile, human expertise is essential for designing strategic campaigns, interpreting complex data results, and making detailed decisions that AI might not be capable of. This collaborative approach leads to more efficient and effective campaign management, as it leverages the computational power of AI and the strategic thinking of humans (Andonians 2023; Davenport 2018; Huang and Rust 2022).

Hybrid intelligence also plays a crucial role in addressing data privacy and ethical issues in marketing. AI technologies can help ensure compliance with privacy regulations, protect customer data, and detect fraudulent activities. However, it is human values that ensure these technologies are used transparently and ethically. By combining AI's capabilities with human oversight, marketing practices can maintain high standards of accountability and trust, aligning with ethical and regulatory requirements (Petrescu and Krishen 2023; SAS 2020).

The collaboration between human intelligence and AI brings substantial advantages to the marketing domain. By combining human intuition and creativity with AI's computational prowess, marketing strategies can be more effectively driven, campaign performances can be enhanced, and customer experiences can be deeply personalised. This hybrid approach is a powerful tool that can develop and change the field of marketing, highlighting the importance of exploring its benefits and challenges for strategic and analytical applications (Davenport 2018; Huang and Rust 2018).

The article "7 AI Marketing Trends for 2024 & What They Mean for You"[1] by John Shieldsmith discusses the significant trends in AI that are shaping the future of marketing. Here is a summary:

1. Further refinement of ad targeting: AI enables marketers to improve ad targeting by analysing large datasets to fine-tune their messaging. This trend is expected to continue evolving, resulting in more accurate ads and also raising the standards for successful ads.
2. Improved AI marketing automation: AI-driven automation is advancing, allowing for quicker pivots, more micro-campaigns, and delivering to smaller segments. This evolution will lead to higher audience expectations for timely and personalised campaigns.
3. More capable chatbots: Advances in AI are enhancing chatbots' abilities to handle nuanced customer questions, guiding users through

websites and sales funnels more effectively. This trend encourages companies to implement advanced chatbots to stay competitive.

4. More use of predictive analytics: Predictive analytics, which forecasts market trends and customer actions based on data, is becoming more sophisticated. This technology will continue to expand, providing better product recommendations and sales forecasts.

5. Improved research and decision-making: AI aids smaller businesses by expediting research and decision-making processes. This levels the playing field, allowing smaller companies to compete with larger ones.

6. Continued adoption of voice-based shopping: As AI advances, voice-based search and shopping will become more prevalent. Marketers need to optimise content for voice search to meet the growing consumer use of voice-activated devices.

7. More use of multimodal AI: Multimodal AI, which combines text, visuals, and other inputs, is becoming more popular. This technology helps companies produce higher volumes of content and more refined ad targeting, enabling smaller businesses to compete with larger teams.

These trends highlight the increasing usage practices of AI in marketing strategies, underlying the need for marketers to adapt to this development to maintain a competitive edge.

When it comes to chatbots, which are broadly used in communication with a client, early chatbots relied on simple keyword matching, but advancements in technology have greatly enhanced their capabilities. Modern chatbots use data mining, machine learning, and linguistic tools, leading to widespread commercial use (Shawar and Atwell 2007). They support human-like interactions across various modalities and assist users in tasks such as asking questions and conducting transactions, although they still struggle with complex queries and long conversations (Jurafsky 2018; Wołk et al. 2022).

Chatbots are classified based on their response mechanisms into rule-based and generative models (Gao 2021; Huang 2021). Wahde and Virgolin (2022) further categorise them into pattern-based, information-retrieval, and generative chatbots. Pattern-based chatbots use predefined templates, information-retrieval chatbots select responses from a corpus, and generative chatbots create responses using deep neural networks.

Another classification is based on the knowledge domain, with open-ended chatbots capable of handling various subjects, and closed-ended ones specific to particular domains (Nicolescu and Tudorache 2022). Despite advancements, open-domain chatbots often produce vague responses (Adiwardana et al. 2020).

Chatbots also vary by interaction type, such as customer service, personal assistants, content curation, and coaching (Nicolescu and Tudorache 2022). Effective collaboration between humans and AI can improve business efficiency, requiring companies to adapt processes to maximise this synergy (Skubis and Wodarski 2023). Chatbots are widely utilised due to their capacity to provide 24/7 customer support at a significantly lower cost, offering immediate responses to most customer inquiries. Additionally, chatbots are cost-effective to train, operate, and customise, including the addition of multiple languages (Wołk et al. 2021).

Despite the recognised importance of AI in marketing, debates continue about whether AI should augment or replace human roles. Some studies suggest replacement, citing consumer perceptions of warmth towards anthropomorphised robots and their impact on consumer attachment and willingness to pay. Conversely, other studies support augmentation, pointing to differences between frontline employees and AI in areas like service training, customer experience, and societal impact. Additionally, consumer resistance to medical AI indicates a need for human mediation. These discussions highlight concerns about AI's role in marketing, focusing on the balance between replacing human marketers and enhancing their capabilities (Huang and Rust 2022).

3.2 AI IN ADVERTISING

The advertising industry has experienced a profound transformation, fundamentally driven by the relentless advancements in technology, particularly through the introduction of artificial intelligence. Initially marked by the digitalisation of traditional media channels, this development allowed advertisements to migrate online, significantly expanding the ability to target audiences through the internet, as noted by Keke (2022). This evolution set the stage for more sophisticated advertising strategies that influence the power of digital platforms.

As the industry grew, it moved into a phase of datafication, with data collection and analysis becoming central to advertising strategies. This phase enabled marketers to create highly targeted and personalised campaigns based on in-depth information about consumer behaviours, thus enhancing the ability to influence consumer decisions and preferences.

The current phase of the advertising industry is intelligence-driven, characterised by the crucial role of AI. According to Alghamdi and Agag (2023), intelligent algorithms now manage search engine advertising, facilitating dynamic ad placements tailored to individual user preferences. This has led to higher click-through and conversion rates, showing the effectiveness of AI in optimising advertising strategies.

The concept of "omnimedia survival", as explained by Cao (2021), further illustrates the pervasive influence of AI. In this approach, every digital platform can serve as a potential channel for delivering targeted messages, with AI-powered technologies like voice recognition and natural language processing enhancing the reach and efficacy of these messages across various media forms.

Many people nowadays search for products mostly on their phones, not computers. Mobile advertising refers to any form of advertising that targets users on mobile devices such as smartphones and tablets. The mobile advertising market is experiencing rapid expansion, with projections indicating that global mobile ad spending will reach $649 billion by 2025. This trend reflects the growing dependence on mobile devices for accessing information and entertainment, compelling businesses to devote more resources to mobile advertising strategies that effectively engage users, according to research by Allam & Jones (2021) and Jebarajakirthy et al. (2021).

The technological innovations such as virtual reality (VR) and augmented reality (AR) has further enhanced the advertising branch, enabling more precise targeting and immersive user experiences (Sutherland et al. 2019). Nowadays, the mobile platforms and mobile applications offer interactive advertising experiences that not only engage users more deeply but also increase monetisation potential by encouraging spontaneous interactions with ad content (Rialti et al. 2022).

AI's role in advertising extends beyond just targeting and placement. It is increasingly employed for personalisation, content creation, and ad optimisation, as detailed by Xia et al. (2023), Bhatt (2021), Campbell et al. (2022), Jaiwant (2023), Malthouse & Copulsky (2023), and Nikolajeva & Teilans (2021). These AI applications analyse consumer behaviour, providing valuable information that enable advertisers to formulate more effective strategies, thus enhancing advertisement information processing and decision-making. For example, McDonald's makes use of AI to optimise its ad targeting by analysing real-time data such as weather conditions and restaurant traffic, thereby dynamically adapting menu board presentations in advertisements to better match customer needs (Haleem et al. 2022).

In the realm of personalisation, advanced AI technologies support personalised recommendation systems that have become indispensable for internet giants like Amazon, YouTube, Netflix, Yahoo, and Facebook, helping them deliver ad content that aligns more closely with individual user preferences (Xia et al. 2023; Laux et al. 2022; Nikolajeva and Teilans 2021; Zhang et al. 2021).

Generative AI has also significantly reduced the barriers to entry for creating diverse and engaging advertising content. By analysing vast amounts of data, generative AI helps creative teams generate varied and rich content, enhancing the quality and impact of advertisements (Wiredu 2023; C. Zhang et al. 2023). The usage of generative AI in advertising will be discussed in Chapter 4.

Moreover, ad optimisation techniques such as deep learning and reinforcement learning tailor advertisements more closely to users' actual needs, in this way improving advertisement efficacy and user purchase conversion rates (Mühlhoff and Willem 2023; Nikolajeva and Teilans 2021; X. Zhang et al. 2017).

Artificial intelligence is applied across different aspects of advertising (e.g. Guo and Jiang 2023; Adriel 2024[2]; The AI Agency[3]; Dimitrieska 2024):

1. AI Ad generation
AI ad generation uses AI tools to automatically create advertising content. These tools can produce text, images, and even video content based on input parameters and learned patterns. For instance, AI can analyse successful past advertisements and generate new ones that mimic these successful elements. It efficiently completes the processes of segmenting, targeting, and personalising content for consumers based on vast datasets. This technology helps to reduce the workload of people, enabling them to concentrate on strategy and innovative concepts while leaving routine production to AI. AI tools like OpenAI's DALL-E and GPT are examples of technologies that generate images and text, respectively.

2. Programmatic creative
Programmatic creative involves the use of AI to automate the decision-making process in ad creative deployment. It combines creative production with data insights to dynamically tailor advertisements to the audience in real time. This approach not only automates ad buying but also ensures that the creatives are optimised for the target audience based on real-time feedback and data analytics. Ad platforms such as Google Ads and Facebook utilise programmatic creative tools to adjust ads based on user interaction and engagement metrics.

3. Ad personalisation
Ad personalisation is the process of tailoring ads to individual users based on their behaviour, preferences, and demographics. AI analyses large datasets to understand patterns and preferences at an individual level, enabling advertisers

to serve highly relevant ads. For example, an e-commerce site might use AI to display ads for products similar to what a user has viewed or added to their cart. Companies like Amazon and Netflix extensively use AI to personalise ads and recommendations to improve user experience and engagement.

4. Predictive snalytics
Predictive analytics in advertising involves using AI to forecast future consumer behaviours based on historical data. This can include predicting trends, user engagement levels, and the potential success of certain ad formats or content. By understanding these patterns, advertisers can pre-emptively adjust their strategies to capitalise on predicted changes or user needs. Tools such as SAS and IBM Watson offer sophisticated predictive analytics capabilities that help businesses model and predict customer behaviours.

5. Ad campaign optimisation
AI in ad campaign optimisation focuses on improving the performance of advertising campaigns through automated analysis and adjustments. AI algorithms can continuously analyse campaign performance data – such as click-through rates, conversion rates, and engagement – and make real-time adjustments to improve outcomes. This might involve changing the audience, modifying the ad spend, or tweaking the ad copy. Platforms like AdRoll and Adobe Advertising Cloud use AI to optimise ad campaigns across various channels and platforms, ensuring maximum Return of Investment for advertisers.

These AI applications are significantly improving the capabilities of advertisers by making campaigns more targeted, efficient, and creative, leading to better results and higher satisfaction among consumers.

As indicated earlier, AI significantly enhances business content creation and personalisation by generating tailored text, images, videos, and full marketing campaigns based on extensive consumer data. It effectively segments and targets content, predicting and meeting individual consumer needs, which boosts engagement, loyalty, and sales conversion rates. According to a McKinsey Report 2023, these AI applications can increase company productivity by 5–15% of total marketing spend. Notable examples include Netflix's personalised movie suggestions, Amazon's custom shopping advice, The New York Times' individualised homepages, and Sephora's targeted cosmetic offers, all of which demonstrate AI's ability to improve content relevance and customer satisfaction (Dimitrieska 2024).

According to 2024 research by Mint (in Dimitrieska 2024), 92% of companies recognise AI's primary benefit as elevating the efficiency of current processes. This is achieved through advanced automation and robotisation, freeing managers for strategic tasks. AI handles routine tasks and provides intelligent solutions for informed decision-making. In budgeting, AI swiftly analyses financial data to identify trends and offer spending and saving recommendations. Kaput (2024) notes AI's capability to evaluate ad performance on various platforms, suggesting improvements and adapting to market changes in real time. AI also optimises advertising budgets through predictive analytics, anticipating consumer behaviour and trends, which aids in customer segmentation and insight modelling (in Dimitrieska 2024).

Regarding audience engagement, Howarth (2024) highlights challenges faced by companies, with 70% of GenZ using generative AI tools and 95% of customer interactions expected to involve AI by 2025. Companies must engage consumers effectively, leveraging AI to deliver dynamic, personalised content based on extensive data analysis. Technologies like AR and VR are being used to create immersive experiences, significantly enhancing customer interaction (Dimitrieska et al. 2024). Additionally, AI aids businesses in media buying, building detailed audience profiles, gaining insights into competitors, and predicting ad effectiveness, among other functions (Kaput 2024).

In summary, the evolution of the advertising industry, marked by the appearance and development of cutting-edge technologies, especially AI, has not only enhanced the effectiveness of advertising strategies but also necessitated continuous adaptation to keep pace with changing consumer behaviours and technological advancements. This ongoing change promises to further shape the future of advertising, including more AI-driven solutions like generative AI for content creation, and tackling emerging challenges such as algorithmic bias, data privacy issues, and ethical considerations in digital advertising.

NOTES

1. Retrieved July 16, 2024, from https://www.wordstream.com/blog/ai-marketing-trends-2024.
2. Retrieved July 18 2024, from https://www.adriel.com/blog/the-future-of-advertising-is-ai.
3. Retrieved July 18 2024, from https://theaiagency.io/ai-marketing/ai-advertising/.

Generative AI

4

The term "generative AI" is defined by EDPS (2024) as follows:

> Generative AI is a subset of AI that uses specialised machine learning models designed to produce wide and general variety of outputs, capable of a range of tasks and applications, such as generating text, image or audio. Concretely, it relies on the use of the so-called foundation models, which serve as baseline models for other generative AI systems that will be "finetuned" from them.

It means that generative AI, also called GenAI, is a branch of artificial intelligence that focuses on creating diverse outputs using specialised machine learning models, known as foundation models. These foundation models provide the underlying architecture upon which more specific applications are developed and fine-tuned. Trained on vast and varied datasets, these models are capable of replicating complex structures such as images, audio, video, and language. Large language models (LLMs), a subset of foundation models, are particularly noteworthy for their ability to generate text based on immense textual data sourced from the internet and other public domains.

Large language models like PALM, LLaMA, GPT-3.5, and GPT-4 have advanced significantly, tackling complex natural language processing (NLP) tasks and even non-NLP challenges such as maths problem solving and code writing, garnering significant attention from various sectors. Despite their capabilities, issues like errors in text generation, unwarranted confidence in incorrect answers, and the production of harmful content remain concerns. OpenAI's use of reinforcement learning with human feedback (RLHF) aims to address these issues, but systematic analysis of their factual limitations is still needed. The rise of generative AI (Gen-AI) systems, including ChatGPT models, marks an essential point in multiple scientific disciplines, with their widespread use sparking debates over academic integrity and their overall impact on various fields (Brown et al. 2020; Khatun and Brown 2023; Sánchez-Ruiz et al. 2023).

Large language models are advanced neural network models that are essential in processing and generating sequential data, such as human language and other forms of "text" like protein sequences or computer code.

DOI: 10.1201/9781003566441-4

According to Bubeck et al. (2023) and Eloundou et al. (2023), LLMs are trained by predicting the next word in a sequence based on vast amounts of textual data sourced from repositories like Wikipedia or digitised books. This training helps them to grasp the statistical co-occurrence of words, enabling the generation of new text that is both grammatically sound and semantically coherent (Brynjolfsson et al. 2023)

Recent advancements in generative AI, which encompass LLMs, have been primarily driven by four factors: increased computing scale, innovations in model architecture, the ability to pre-train using extensive unlabeled data, and refined training techniques. The progression in computing power, as noted by Kaplan et al. (2020), directly correlates with the quality of LLMs; for example, the transition from GPT-3 to GPT-4 showed a marked increase in parameters and training data, which significantly raised both the costs and capabilities of these models (Li 2020; Brown et al. 2020; Patel and Wong 2023).

Technological innovations such as positional encoding and self-attention mechanisms, detailed by Vaswani et al. (2017) and Bahdanau et al. (2015), are crucial in maintaining the sequential context and assigning relevance across the input text. These advancements allow LLMs to manage and interpret extensive and complex text segments effectively, enhancing their ability to maintain coherence over longer stretches of text (Brynjolfsson et al. 2023).

Moreover, LLMs significantly benefit from pre-training on large datasets of unlabeled data, which is far more abundant than labelled data. This aspect of their training allows them to develop a nuanced understanding of language patterns and relationships without the need for direct guidance, as highlighted by Radford and Narasimhan (2018). Once the general training is complete, LLMs can be fine-tuned for specific applications, making them versatile tools for a variety of tasks – from generating social media content to responding to user queries in a contextually appropriate manner (Ouyang et al. 2022; Liu et al. 2023).

Applications of generative AI are wide-ranging and include code generation, virtual assistants, content creation tools, language translation, automated speech recognition, and even medical diagnostic systems. The hierarchical relationship between the broad category of generative AI, foundation models, and specialised models underscores a structured approach to AI development. Each phase of a generative AI model's life cycle, from initial use case definition to deployment and continuous evaluation, involves significant planning and customisation to ensure alignment with specific tasks or applications (EDPS 2024).

Generative AI has made significant strides across numerous industries, transforming traditional processes and enabling new capabilities. In the following, we present diverse applications of generative AI, highlighting its impact and potential in various sectors.

1. Healthcare

Generative AI has introduced many changes in healthcare by enhancing diagnostic accuracy, personalising treatment plans, and optimising operational efficiencies. One prominent application is in medical imaging, where AI models like those used in low-dose computed tomography (CT) image denoising significantly improve image quality while reducing radiation exposure for patients (Marcos et al. 2024). Additionally, generative models are employed for drug discovery, simulating molecular structures and predicting the efficacy of new compounds, thereby accelerating the development of new medications (Revell 2024). Generative AI is used, but not limited to, in the following sectors:

2. Finance

In the financial sector, generative AI is used to create investment strategies, draft documentation, and monitor regulatory changes. AI models analyse market trends and historical data to recommend optimal investment opportunities, offering a competitive edge to financial institutions (Chen et al. 2020). Furthermore, generative AI assists in drafting complex financial documents and keeping abreast of regulatory updates, streamlining compliance processes and reducing manual labour (Ozbayoglu et al. 2020).

3. Media and entertainment

The media and entertainment industry benefits significantly from generative AI through content creation and personalisation. AI can generate new video content, create visual effects, and edit media faster than traditional methods (Elgammal et al. 2017). Platforms like Synthesia enable the creation of personalised video content at scale, improving marketing and communication efforts. Moreover, AI-driven tools can generate highlight reels for sports events, manage extensive media libraries, and even produce creative works such as music and poetry.

4. Manufacturing and construction

Generative AI in manufacturing and construction improves design processes, predictive maintenance, and supply chain management. AI models generate design ideas and assess their feasibility based on project constraints, accelerating the design phase.

In manufacturing, GenAI is utilised to streamline production processes, enhance product design, and improve supply chain logistics. By generating and simulating countless design iterations, GenAI facilitates rapid prototyping and innovation, allowing manufacturers to explore a wider array of product designs and material compositions with reduced physical and financial constraints. Predictive maintenance is another critical application, where AI models predict equipment failures before they occur, thus minimising downtime and extending machinery life (Westphal and Seitz 2024; SCW AI 2024).

In construction, the adoption of GenAI is transforming traditional practices, particularly in design and project management. AI-driven tools assist in creating more efficient building designs by automatically generating layouts that comply with regulatory constraints and optimising them for environmental and operational efficiency. Furthermore, these tools enhance collaboration among different stakeholders by providing platforms that integrate and visualise changes dynamically, facilitating faster consensus and decision-making processes (Ghimire, Kim and Acharya 2024; Taiwo et al. 2024).

5. Education
In education, generative AI creates personalised learning experiences, adapts educational content, and assists in administrative tasks. AI models can generate customised lesson plans and assessments tailored to individual student needs, enhancing learning outcomes (Zawacki-Richter et al. 2019). Furthermore, AI helps automate administrative processes such as grading and scheduling, allowing educators to focus more on teaching.

6. Software development
Generative AI significantly impacts software development by automating code generation, translating programming languages, and optimising testing processes. Tools like GitHub Copilot assist developers by suggesting code snippets and completing code blocks, speeding up the development process (Allamanis et al. 2018). AI-driven automated testing improves software quality by identifying potential issues and executing test cases efficiently.

7. Marketing
In marketing, generative AI enhances content creation, personalisation, and strategy development. AI tools generate marketing assets such as emails, social media posts, and ad creatives, ensuring consistent brand voice and tone (Davenport and Ronanki 2018). Personalised marketing strategies are developed by analysing customer data, allowing for targeted and effective campaigns. AI also assists in content localisation, making it easier to reach global audiences (Jarek and Mazurek 2019).

Generative AI continues to evolve, driving innovation across various industries and offering new opportunities for efficiency and creativity. As technology advances, its applications will undoubtedly expand, further integrating AI into our daily lives and professional environments.

4.1 GENERATIVE AI IN ADVERTISING

The field of advertising has enormously changed with the appearance of artificial intelligence, which has emerged as a transformative force, driving innovations that reshape how brands connect with consumers. Among the various AI technologies, generative AI stands out, offering unparalleled capabilities in content creation, personalisation, and real-time decision-making. This technology uses algorithms to generate text, images, videos, and other media that were traditionally created by humans. The aim to create an appealing advertisement can be done from simple prompts, suggesting a significant step forward in creative and operational processes within the industry (Lawton 2023; Loten 2023; Cellerin 2023; Muliyil 2023).

Major corporations like Google, Amazon, Meta, and Microsoft are integrating GenAI into their advertising strategies, a move indicative of the technology's growing influence and anticipated market growth, which is expected to exceed $109 billion by 2030 (Grand View Research 2023).

As digitalisation becomes more complex and consumer behaviours change unpredictably, generative AI provides advertisers with the agility and creativity necessary to stay relevant and compelling. Moreover, generative AI is revolutionising digital advertising by enhancing creativity, efficiency, and personalisation. It produces innovative, human-like content, bridging the gap between human and machine-generated creativity and transforming industry collaboration. GAI enables the creation of highly personalised ad content, improving engagement and conversion rates through deep data analysis that emotionally connects with consumers. Users receive customised advertisements and offers in real-time based on their engagement activities such as views, likes, comments, and other interactions.

The quick expansion of AI has led to the development of sophisticated conversational models that can engage in natural and meaningful dialogues with users. Among these, GPT by OpenAI, Bard by Google, and Bing Chat by Microsoft stand out due to their unique approaches and widespread applications. Moreover, due to their capabilities of writing good texts, they became the source of inspirations for marketers and advertisers or even more, they go beyond being a source of inspiration, they prepare the whole advertisements.

The three most known and used AI models are as follows:

- GPT (generative pre-trained transformer): Developed by OpenAI, GPT models, including GPT-3.5 and GPT-4, leverage transformer architectures with extensive pre-training on diverse datasets. They are known for their versatility and coherence in generating human-like text. GPT-4, in particular, has shown remarkable improvements in contextual understanding and response generation, surpassing previous benchmarks in NLP tasks (Brown et al. 2020; OpenAI[1]).
- Gemini (previously Bard): Before the Gemini models, Google's Bard served as a significant predecessor. Bard used earlier versions of AI models and focused on creative text generation, making significant contributions to conversational AI development. With the introduction of Gemini, the capabilities have been expanded and enhanced to provide even more advanced and efficient AI solutions (Google Blog,[2] DeepMind[3]). Gemini is Google's latest and most advanced AI model family, designed to be highly versatile and capable of running efficiently on a wide range of devices, from data centres to mobile phones. Developed by Google DeepMind, Gemini represents a significant leap in AI technology, offering state-of-the-art capabilities across multiple modalities including text, images, audio, and video.
- Copilot (previously Bing): In February 2023, Microsoft introduced a new AI-enhanced Bing service that improves web search by summarising search results and providing a chat feature. Users can also create content like poems, jokes, stories, and images with the Bing image creator. The service incorporates advanced technologies from Microsoft and OpenAI, including GPT for language processing and DALL-E for image generation. After months of development and customisation, Microsoft released this service, integrating cutting-edge AI with web search. In November 2023, Microsoft rebranded the service as Copilot in Bing (Microsoft[4]).

As indicated by Gujar and Panyam (2024), GAI automates content production, allowing brands to quickly generate large volumes of tailored content, adapting rapidly to market trends and consumer preferences. This automation reduces the need for extensive creative teams and shortens production timelines, enabling more effective resource allocation. However, GAI faces challenges in capturing a brand's unique identity and ensuring content aligns with brand values and ethical standards. Editing GAI-generated content can be difficult due to potential inconsistencies and biases. Privacy concerns also arise from GAI's deep data usage. Despite these challenges, GAI, integrated with cloud technologies, enhances capabilities with increased computational power and data security, setting new standards for creativity and efficiency in advertising while demanding careful oversight to respect consumer privacy and brand integrity.

ChatGPT, a prominent GenAI tool, exemplifies this advancement by offering superior natural language processing capabilities. Since its release in November 2022, ChatGPT has attracted 100 million monthly users in just two months, marking it as the fastest-growing consumer application in history (Hu, 2023). Its rapid adoption highlights its potential to significantly impact advertising, though opinions vary on the extent of this impact – from transformative to merely incremental (Osadchaya et al. 2024; Fischer 2023; Kulp 2023; Clugston 2023).

The paradoxical nature of technology, as discussed by Gebauer et al. (2020), Mick and Fournier (1998), and Sirkka and Lang (2005), suggests that while GenAI offers considerable opportunities, it also presents challenges that need careful investigation. For example, it can foster both independence and dependence or intelligence and ignorance, highlighting the complex dualities that professionals must manage (Lewis 2000). Advertisers must recognise these paradoxes – operational and psychological – to benefit from GenAI effectively and secure competitive advantages (Berthon et al. 2024; Osadchaya et al. 2024; Ferraro et al. 2024; Pedersen 2023).

4.2 CHATGPT AND ITS FEATURES

In recent years, the field of artificial intelligence has witnessed significant changes, especially in the domain of natural language processing. Among these developments, conversational AI has appeared as a critical area of research and application, driven by the growing demand for more intuitive and effective human-computer interactions (HCIs).

As large language models like OpenAI's ChatGPT become more accessible, generative artificial intelligence has changed our work and life. Academia and the public have shown both concern and excitement about this technology (Botha and Pieterse 2020; Clayton 2023; Haupt and Marks 2023; Khan 2023; Li et al. 2023), and there is interest in how GAI like ChatGPT will impact businesses and industries (Berg et al. 2023; Zhang 2023).

ChatGPT, developed by OpenAI, stands at the forefront of this innovation, representing a major breakthrough in conversational AI capabilities. OpenAI uses deep learning to train AI systems with vast data, enhancing their understanding and processing abilities. They lead research into artificial general intelligence (AGI) to solve human-level problems. Their advanced text models excel in generating, classifying, and summarising text with high coherence and accuracy, producing high-quality, contextually relevant outputs.

ChatGPT was developed through a two-phase process: unsupervised pre-training and supervised fine-tuning. In pre-training, the model was exposed to a vast corpus of text data to understand natural language structure and relationships. Fine-tuning further optimised the model using labelled datasets for specific tasks, adjusting parameters to minimise discrepancies (Radford and Narasimhan 2018; Radford et al. 2019; Roumeliotis and Tselikas 2023).

ChatGPT, built on the GPT (generative pre-trained transformer) architecture, is engineered to understand and generate human-like text based on the input it receives. This model has not only captivated the scientific community but has also found practical applications across a myriad of industries. From automating customer service interactions to assisting in complex programming tasks, ChatGPT's versatility is evident in its wide-ranging utility.

The importance of ChatGPT extends beyond its immediate functionality. As a conversational model, it challenges the traditional boundaries between human and machine communication, offering a glimpse into the future of AI where machines can understand and respond to human needs with unprecedented accuracy and relevance.

Till now, it was said that communication is the most important part of human interaction (Skubis 2022a); however nowadays, when we often communicate with computers, proper communication with machines is also an important part of our lives and is called human-machine interaction (HMI), human-computer interaction (HCI), or when it comes to communication with robots human-robot interaction. Research indicates GAI can also enhance labour productivity in areas such as customer communication (Brynjolfsson et al. 2023).

In communication, Guo et al. (2023) highlighted ChatGPT's potential in semantic importance communication, showing lower error rates and semantic losses when embedded in communication systems.

In order to communicate with ChatGPT, some essential terminology needs to be introduced. First, the term "prompt". The prompt is a set of specific instructions given to a conversational large language model (LLM) to tailor or enhance its performance. It determines the nature of the LLM's responses by setting the context, specifying what information is crucial, and defining the desired form and content of the output. For instance, a prompt can direct an LLM to adhere to a particular coding style or to highlight and expand on specific keywords in its responses. The second term that needs to be mentioned is "prompt engineering". This process optimises the LLM's utility, particularly in complex software engineering tasks, by enabling more structured and detailed outputs (White et al. 2023).

On the OpenAI website, the GPT model is described as trained to comprehend both natural language and code, producing responses to user-provided inputs known as "prompts". OpenAI defines the creation of these prompts as a way of "programming" the GPT model by offering specific instructions or examples to guide the model in completing tasks effectively. This process of crafting prompts in natural language is termed "prompt engineering", "prompt programming", "prompt design", or simply "prompting" (Oppenlaender 2022).

OpenAI gives us the following instructions for using prompts with ChatGPT:[5]

1. Use latest models: Newer models are easier to prompt engineer.
2. Clear instructions: Place instructions at the beginning, separated by ### or ".
3. Be specific: Clearly define context, outcome, length, format, and style.
4. Use examples: Show specific format requirements to aid model response.
5. Zero-shot to few-shot to fine-tune: Start with zero-shot, provide examples for few-shot, and fine-tune if necessary.
6. Avoid fluffy descriptions: Use precise, concise instructions.
7. Positive instructions: Specify what to do rather than what not to do.
8. Code generation: Use leading words to guide the model.

Bang et al. (2023) explored the capabilities and limitations of ChatGPT, identifying several challenges such as failures in elementary mathematical tasks, issues with common sense reasoning, and tendencies to hallucinate. To address these concerns, they proposed an evaluation framework in February 2023 for assessing interactive large language models (LLMs) like ChatGPT using public test sets across various NLP tasks, including question answering, reasoning, summarisation, and more. They made analysis in the following categories: multitask, multimodal, and multilingual performance; reasoning abilities; hallucinations; and interactivity. The outcomes of their research are described in the following:

1. Multitask performance: ChatGPT demonstrated remarkable zero-shot performance across multiple tasks, outperforming previous state-of-the-art (SOTA) zero-shot models on 9 out of 13 evaluation datasets. In some tasks, particularly task-oriented and knowledge-grounded dialogue, ChatGPT even surpassed fully fine-tuned models. However, it performed lower than fine-tuned models in other specific NLP tasks. For instance, in summarisation, ChatGPT's

ability to generate concise and readable summaries was enhanced through interactive prompt engineering, achieving significant improvements in ROUGE scores after iterative feedback.

2. Multimodal performance: Although ChatGPT is primarily a text-based model, it displayed basic multimodal capabilities by generating code-based visual representations, such as Scalable Vector Graphics (SVG) images, from textual descriptions. In a national flag drawing task, ChatGPT showed the ability to create plausible visual outputs through an iterative process of generating descriptions and refining images based on feedback. However, it struggled with more complex visual details, indicating that while it has emergent multimodal abilities, there is room for improvement compared to dedicated vision-language models.

3. Multilingual performance: ChatGPT exhibited strong performance in high-resource and medium-resource languages but struggled significantly with low-resource languages. The model was better at understanding non-Latin scripts than generating them. For example, it performed well in sentiment analysis and language identification tasks in high-resource languages like English and Chinese but showed notable performance degradation in low-resource languages such as Javanese and Sundanese. The evaluation also revealed that ChatGPT could generate English translations of high quality from high-resource languages but produced less accurate translations for low-resource languages and sometimes even hallucinated content.

4. Reasoning abilities: ChatGPT's reasoning abilities varied across different categories. It showed weaknesses in inductive reasoning, mathematical reasoning, and multi-hop reasoning but performed better in temporal reasoning and common-sense reasoning. Despite its ability to handle some logical reasoning tasks, ChatGPT's overall reliability in reasoning remains questionable, requiring further development to enhance its capabilities in complex reasoning tasks.

5. Hallucinations: Similar to other LLMs, ChatGPT exhibited issues with hallucinations, generating factual statements that could not be verified. This problem was evident across various tasks, including machine translation and question answering, where it produced both untruthful and extrinsic hallucinations.

6. Interactivity: One of ChatGPT's primary strengths is its interactivity, which allows for human collaboration to improve its performance. Through multi-turn dialogue, users can refine the model's outputs, leading to significant improvements in tasks such as summaries and

machine translation. This interactive feature sets ChatGPT apart from previous LLMs, enabling it to adapt and enhance its responses based on user feedback.

In the medical field, ChatGPT has shown promising applications for question-answering and diagnosis assistance. Nov et al. (2023) conducted an experiment using ChatGPT for patient-doctor communication, where ChatGPT answered patient questions with accuracy comparable to doctors, although patients showed slightly lower trust in responses for complex health questions. Tu et al. (2023) examined ChatGPT's capability in diagnosing neuropathic pain, noting limitations in understanding new medical knowledge beyond its training data, along with issues in response consistency.

Zhang and Gosline (2023) conducted an analysis which is valuable to our research. Their study examined how people perceive content generated by humans, AI, and human-AI interactions. Previous research focused solely on content created by humans or AI, not considering collaborative human-AI efforts. For example, Ayers et al. (2023) found that ChatGPT-generated medical responses were rated higher in quality than those by physicians, but real-life scenarios often involve combined efforts of humans and AI.

Their research compared the quality of persuasive content generated under four paradigms:

1. Human expert-only
2. AI-only (ChatGPT-4)
3. Augmented human (human experts refine AI-generated content)
4. Augmented AI (AI refines human-generated content)

Participants rated content without knowing its origin (baseline), being partially informed, or fully informed about the content generation process. Results showed that content generated solely or ultimately by ChatGPT-4 was perceived as higher quality. Surprisingly, this perception held even when participants were informed about the content's AI origin, contradicting the "algorithm aversion" literature (Castelo et al. 2019; Dietvorst et al. 2015).

Moreover, Zhang and Gosline (2023) found that people rated human-generated content higher only when they knew it was created solely by humans, indicating a bias towards human expertise. Their findings highlight the importance of understanding public perception and bias in the adoption of AI-generated content.

This research provides valuable data on the human-AI collaboration in content generation and how this cooperation is perceived, and it suggests that people may favour human involvement, even if AI can produce high-quality content on its own.

4.3 ETHICS OF GENERATIVE AI

The ethical considerations surrounding the usage of AI technologies such as ChatGPT are very complex and unambiguous, prompting a wide range of academic scrutiny and proposal of regulatory measures.

One of the main concerns associated with the development of artificial intelligence is safety and responsibility. Ensuring AI safety involves creating systems that operate reliably and predictably, minimising risks and preventing harm. Responsibility encompasses ethical considerations, accountability, and ensuring that AI technologies are developed and used in ways that are fair, transparent, and aligned with societal values. These concerns highlight the need for robust regulatory frameworks, continuous monitoring, and collaboration between stakeholders to address potential risks and ensure the ethical deployment of AI (Skubis 2021; Skubis 2024).

ChatGPT, with its profound capabilities in text generation, causes concerns regarding its potential to facilitate plagiarism and cheating across various sectors including academia, journalism, law, and medicine. Researchers like Zhou et al. (2022) have raised alarms about the ease with which such technology can produce convincing text, potentially heralding the end of traditional paper-based evaluations as reliable assessment tools. This raises concerns in the context of maintaining the credibility of news media and scholarly publications (Liu et al. 2023).

Further complications arise in educational settings, where the technology could be misused to cheat on examinations. Susnjak and McIntosh (2024) suggest that creating examination questions that require critical thinking could mitigate this risk by using ChatGPT's capabilities to foster rather than hinder educational integrity. Despite its potential for generating accurate and persuasive content, educators are encouraged to develop strategies to prevent academic dishonesty to preserve the fairness of online examinations.

On the political and ethical front, studies such as those by Hartmann et al. (2023) have employed tools like Wahl-O-Mat to analyse ChatGPT's ideological biases, revealing a propensity towards environmentally friendly and left-wing liberal stances. Moreover, inconsistencies in moral reasoning have been observed when ChatGPT is tested with ethical dilemmas such as the trolley problem, indicating a lack of firm moral convictions and potentially influencing users' moral judgements.

Zhuo et al. (2023) explore the ethical concerns associated with the use of large language models (LLMs) like ChatGPT, focusing on two primary application scenarios: "creative generation" and "decision-making". In the creative generation scenario, LLMs are used to produce new content, such as stories, poetry, or scripts. These models are trained on vast amounts of text, enabling them to learn patterns and styles, which they can then replicate to generate similar outputs. This application has several downstream uses, including content creation for entertainment, marketing, advertising, and summarisation.

In the decision-making scenario, LLMs assist in making informed decisions based on natural language inputs. They perform tasks like sentiment analysis, text classification, and question answering. By understanding and interpreting the meaning and context of the input, these models can provide judgements or suggestions. This capability is vital for applications in chatbots, virtual assistants, and language-based games.

However, the deployment of LLMs raises several common ethical concerns, which Zhuo et al. (2023) categorise into four main themes: bias, robustness, reliability, and toxicity.

Bias is a significant concern in LLM development and deployment. Social stereotypes and unfair discrimination can arise when the training data contains biased representations of certain groups. For instance, a language technology used for recruitment might inadvertently favour or disadvantage certain groups based on historical biases in the training data. Exclusionary norms occur when a model is trained on data that only represents a fraction of the population, leading to a lack of understanding or generation of content for underrepresented groups. Multilingualism bias happens when models are trained primarily in one language, limiting their ability to serve speakers of other languages. Addressing bias involves ensuring diverse and representative training data and actively identifying and eliminating potential biases.

Robustness refers to a model's ability to maintain performance across varying inputs. Semantic perturbation, where inputs are syntactically different but semantically similar to training data, can cause model failures. Data leakage poses a risk to privacy and security, as sensitive information might be inadvertently exposed during training. Prompt injection, where malicious inputs are designed to disrupt model performance, requires thorough testing and robust security measures to prevent such attacks.

Reliability is another ethical concern, focusing on the model's ability to provide accurate and dependable information. False or misleading information can result from inaccurate or biased training data, leading to erroneous outputs. Outdated information can also be problematic, as models trained on obsolete data may provide irrelevant or incorrect information. Ensuring the accuracy and currency of training data, along with continuous monitoring and updating of the models, is crucial for maintaining reliability.

Toxicity in language models pertains to the generation or understanding of harmful or offensive content. Offensive language in the training data can lead to the production of harmful outputs. Similarly, the presence of pornographic content in the training data can result in inappropriate responses.

Mitigating toxicity involves scrupulously curating the training data to exclude harmful content and actively identifying and removing any such content that may be present.

To address these ethical concerns, Zhuo et al. (2023) stress the importance of using diverse and representative training data, regularly updating models with current data, and implementing robust security measures against malicious inputs. Regular evaluations and transparency about training data and potential biases are essential to maintain the performance and ethical standards of LLMs.

Regulatory discussions have also been prominent, with scholars like Hacker et al. (2023) arguing for comprehensive legislative frameworks that involve all stakeholders in the AI value chain. This approach aims to tailor regulations that safeguard societal interests while fostering innovation and legal clarity in the rapidly evolving domain of AI technology.

The ChatGPT Taskforce's report, created by European Data Protection Board (EDPB), dated May 23, 2024, meticulously examines the ongoing investigations and preliminary findings concerning the compliance of OpenAI's ChatGPT with the General Data Protection Regulation (GDPR). The report highlights the emergence of large language models (LLMs) such as ChatGPT, acknowledging their potential benefits whilst drawing attention to the regulatory challenges they present, particularly in terms of data protection.

A taskforce was established to facilitate cooperation among European supervisory authorities (SAs) to ensure coordinated enforcement actions are directed at privacy concerns associated with ChatGPT. The investigations have primarily focused on scrutinising the privacy policies implemented by OpenAI prior to February 15, 2024, and assessing any compliance measures taken in response to enforcement actions, including a temporary ban in Italy.

The taskforce's preliminary views on several compliance areas are as follows:

1. Lawfulness: Significant concerns have been raised regarding the legality of collecting and processing training data, especially regarding methods like web scraping and the subsequent use of this data under GDPR provisions.
2. Fairness: The taskforce emphasises that data processing should not be detrimental, misleading, or unjustifiably discriminatory against users.
3. Transparency and information obligations: The report identifies challenges in effectively informing data subjects about the use of their data, especially when collected through indirect means such as web scraping.

4. Data accuracy: Given the probabilistic nature of ChatGPT's outputs, the taskforce questions the reliability and accuracy of the information it provides, highlighting that such outputs are often perceived as factually accurate by users.

5. Rights of data subjects: The report underscores the necessity for OpenAI to provide clear and accessible avenues for individuals to exercise their GDPR rights, such as the ability to access, correct, and delete their data.

The report concludes that while the investigations are ongoing, the preliminary views suggest a complex relationship between AI technology and data protection laws. The taskforce recommends a closer alignment of GDPR enforcement with the forthcoming regulations under the EU Artificial Intelligence Act to better manage the unique challenges posed by AI technologies. It recommends continuous review and adaptation of data protection measures to ensure ongoing compliance and protection of individual rights, highlighting the evolving nature of both technology and regulatory frameworks.

On May 13, 2022, the French Council presidency introduced an amendment to the draft AI Act, specifically focusing on "general-purpose AI systems" (GPAIS). This amendment, essential in the direct regulation of large AI models, was heavily debated in the European Parliament (EP) and was central to the ongoing discussions for the AI Act's final version. The Council's definition, from December 6, 2022, categorises GPAIS as systems capable of performing functions like image and speech recognition, among others, in various contexts and as components of other AI systems. Under the Council's guidelines, these systems, if used as or within high-risk systems, must comply with the strict obligations set out in Articles 8 to 15 of the AI Act (Hacker et al. 2023).

The AI Act (2024) mentions "general-purpose AI models" and indicates in point (99) that large generative AI models are prime examples of general-purpose AI, as they can produce diverse types of content – such as text, audio, images, or video – making them adaptable to various tasks. It states in point (105) that they offer significant innovation opportunities and also pose challenges for creators regarding how their work is generated, used, and distributed. Developing these models involves extensive use of text and data, often protected by copyright. While Directive (EU) 2019/790 allows certain text and data mining for research under specific conditions, rights holders can reserve their rights to prevent such activities. If rights are reserved, AI developers must obtain permission from rights holders for text and data mining.

AI ACT (2024) enumerates four types of risks. Some AI systems intended for interaction with people or content generation may pose risks of impersonation or deception without being classified as high-risk. This includes chatbots, such as those based on ChatGPT. These systems are identified as limited-risk AI systems and must adhere to specific transparency obligations. Unlike high-risk systems that require extensive development and risk management measures, the obligations for limited-risk systems focus on their outputs and users. It is essential to inform people when they are interacting with a chatbot. This transparency ensures that users are aware they are communicating with an AI system rather than a human.

Hacker et al. (2023) provide a detailed critique of the GPAIS AI Act rules, arguing that they fall short in addressing the unique challenges posed by large generative AI models (LGAIMs). They identify three primary issues with the current regulations.

Firstly, according to Hacker et al. (2023), the definition of GPAIS in Article 3(1b) of the AI Act is overly broad. This definition fails to distinguish between simple AI models and genuinely general-purpose AI systems. As a result, simpler AI systems that lack the extensive capabilities of LGAIMs could be subjected to inappropriate regulation, which may lead to inefficiencies and misplaced regulatory efforts.

Secondly, the high-risk obligations set out in the AI Act present significant challenges for LGAIMs. These models, due to their versatility, would require a comprehensive risk management system to assess and mitigate risks for every conceivable high-risk application. This requirement is almost unfeasible and could result in wasted resources on hypothetical risks that may never materialise. The authors argue that this approach imposes an impractical burden on providers, who would need to conduct extensive, abstract risk analyses and implement numerous mitigation strategies for all possible high-risk uses.

Thirdly, the current rules could have adverse competitive consequences. The stringent compliance costs associated with the AI Act could be prohibitive for smaller developers and open-source projects, thus favouring large, well-funded companies. This scenario could lead to further market concentration, undermining the objectives of the Digital Markets Act, which aims to foster competition in the digital and platform economy.

The critique also addresses the European Parliament's proposal, which introduces layered obligations for generative AI systems. The EP's approach classifies foundation models as high-risk by default and mandates comprehensive risk assessments, mitigation measures, and transparency obligations. However, the authors argue that these measures remain overly burdensome and could stifle innovation.

Hacker et al. (2023) propose a change in regulatory focus towards the deployers and users of LGAIMs rather than the developers. They suggest that regulatory efforts should concentrate on specific high-risk applications. Furthermore, they advocate for legally mandated collaboration between developers, deployers, and users to meet regulatory requirements effectively.

The authors underline that this approach would ensure that responsibilities are shared across the AI value chain, enabling more practical and targeted compliance.

Additionally, the authors call for a selective expansion of the Digital Services Act (DSA) to address content moderation for LGAIMs. They recommend implementing notice and action mechanisms and involving trusted flaggers to help monitor and mitigate harmful content generated by these models. Hacker et al. (2023) support a more nuanced regulatory approach that balances the need for innovation, competition, and the mitigation of risks associated with LGAIMs. They stress the importance of tailoring regulations to the specific challenges and capabilities of these advanced AI systems, rather than imposing blanket high-risk obligations that could hinder progress and exacerbate market concentration.

Managing innovation in the advertising industry requires balancing stakeholder expectations with ethical considerations in product development. Companies must start with a deep understanding of market needs, using research data, trend analysis, and user feedback to identify gaps and create relevant products. Ethical considerations are crucial, requiring the involvement of ethicists, sociologists, and psychologists to ensure products are designed with various ethical and cultural perspectives in mind. Prototyping and iterative testing help identify potential issues early and adjust designs to meet user expectations. Additionally, managing stakeholder expectations through transparent communication about the capabilities and limitations of new technologies is essential for building trust and setting realistic expectations (Skubis 2024).

In conclusion, while ChatGPT and similar AI technologies offer significant benefits, they also present substantial ethical challenges that necessitate continued research, thoughtful policy-making, and vigilant implementation to ensure they contribute positively and equitably to society.

NOTES

1. Retrieved July 18, 2024, from https://openai.com.
2. Retrieved July 18, 2024, from https://blog.google.
3. Retrieved July 18, 2024, from https://deepmind.google.
4. Retrieved July 18, 2024, from https://learn.microsoft.com/en-us/microsoftsearch/overview-microsoft-search-bing.
5. Retrieved July 18, 2024, from https://help.openai.com/en/articles/6654000-best-practices-for-prompt-engineering-with-open.

The Analysis of Selected Beauty Products Advertisements

5

The following chapter touches upon the study performed especially for the paper to demonstrate the application of the language features described in earlier chapters. The idea behind this study is to check how language encourages recipients of advertisements to buy products. The language of advertising is complex and contains many persuasive and manipulative techniques. These are, in its essence, an inevitable part of consumer's society. The following study was conducted to check whether linguistic features used in the advertisement indeed persuade and manipulate the recipient or it does not have a particular influence on the buyer. The questions raised are as follows:

1. What language features have been applied to attract attention and encourage purchase?
2. Which linguistic level predominates the most in the context of advertising?
3. Is persuasion related to the number of language features used?

The hypotheses suggested for this study are as follows:

1. The language features have been applied on three levels, each of which has characteristics that encourage purchase.
2. The lexical level of language predominates the most in the context of advertising.
3. The number of language features used in the analysed advertisements makes persuasion more effective.

DOI: 10.1201/9781003566441-5

5.1 METHODOLOGY

The analysis presented in this book aims to evaluate and compare the linguistic measures and persuasiveness of advertisements for beauty products created by humans and by AI models, specifically ChatGPT 3.5 and ChatGPT 4.0. The methodology consists of several detailed steps, outlined as follows:

1. **Selection of advertisements**: A variety of beauty product advertisements were selected from reputable brands such as L'Oréal Paris, Avon, The Balm, The Body Shop, Garnier, Janssen Cosmetics, Aesop, and Face Reality. These advertisements cover a broad range of products, including make-up and skin/body/hair care items, ensuring a diverse sample for analysis.

2. **Human-created advertisements analysis:** The first set of advertisements, crafted by humans, was meticulously analysed based on linguistic measures and their persuasiveness. This analysis involved identifying and categorising linguistic features at three distinct levels:
   - **Lexical level**: The examination focused on word choice, including the use of favourable adjectives, neologisms, and weasel words that subtly influence consumer perception.
   - **Syntactic level**: This involved analysing sentence structure, including the use of imperative sentences, parallelism, and the complexity of sentences. The goal was to understand how these structures contribute to the clarity and impact of the message.
   - **Rhetorical level**: The identification of rhetorical devices such as metaphors, personification, and hyperbole was crucial. These devices were evaluated for their role in enhancing the appeal and memorability of the advertisements.

3. **AI-generated advertisements creation and analysis**: Both ChatGPT 3.5 and ChatGPT 4.0 were tasked with generating advertisements for the same beauty products. Each AI model was given a predefined prompt that included specific instructions to use linguistic measures from the semantic, syntactic, and rhetorical levels. After generating the advertisements, the AI models were asked to enumerate and describe the linguistic measures they used.

   The advertisements generated by ChatGPT 3.5 and ChatGPT 4.0 were then subjected to a detailed analysis. This analysis was similar to that of the human-crafted advertisements, focusing on the use of linguistic measures and evaluating the persuasiveness of the AI-generated content.

4. **Evaluation of AI recognition and usage of linguistic measures**: A critical part of the methodology was to evaluate the accuracy and effectiveness of the linguistic measures recognised and utilised by ChatGPT 3.5 and ChatGPT 4.0. This involved assessing whether the AI models accurately identified and applied the specified linguistic measures and how these measures impacted the overall persuasiveness of the advertisements.

5. **Comparative analysis**: A comprehensive comparative analysis was conducted to highlight the differences and similarities between the advertisements created by humans and those generated by ChatGPT 3.5 and ChatGPT 4.0. This comparison aimed to demonstrate the strengths and weaknesses of human versus AI-generated advertisements in terms of linguistic features and their overall effectiveness.

   The analysis included examining the effectiveness of linguistic features and their impact on persuasiveness across different sets of advertisements. By doing so, it aimed to provide insights into the evolving landscape of advertising with the integration of AI technologies.

6. **Results and findings**: The findings from the analysis were compiled to present a thorough understanding of the application of linguistic features in advertising language and the role of AI in this domain. The results highlighted the strengths and weaknesses of human-crafted and AI-generated advertisements, offering valuable information for researchers, marketers, and AI developers.

   The results demonstrated the nuances in how humans and AI approach the creation of persuasive advertisements and the implications for the future of advertising. This comprehensive understanding aimed to guide future developments and applications in the field of AI-driven marketing and advertising.

This methodology provides a structured approach to analysing and comparing the linguistic measures and persuasiveness of beauty product advertisements created by humans and AI. By following these detailed steps, the study aims to offer valuable and practical information for researchers, marketers, and AI developers, contributing to the broader understanding of advertising language and the growing influence of AI in this field.

5.2 RESULTS

The data are collected by choosing the fragments or phrases from various beauty products advertisements which show some linguistic features with persuasion and manipulation effects. The following analysis of chosen advertisements demonstrates the application of the language features described in earlier chapters. Advertisements for beauty products from internet websites such as L'Oréal Paris, Avon, The Balm, The Body Shop, Garnier, Janssen Cosmetics, Aesop, and Face Reality were investigated and divided into two groups – make-up and skin/body/hair care products.

1. Make-up products

Example 1

a. Advertisement made by a human

**BOX 5.1   L'ORÉAL PARIS, FOUNDATION –
ADVERTISEMENT BY A HUMAN**

Our Infallible 32H Freshwear Foundation in 20 Ivory, with vitamin C and SPF25. A transfer-proof and water-proof foundation with full coverage so you get more from your makeup. The innovative oxygen technology gives a lightweight feel whilst the ultra-stretchable formula ensures full coverage application, so a little goes a long way. Life doesn't compromise, so now your makeup doesn't either.

In this particular example, it can be observed that the advertisement makes extensive use of linguistic features at the lexical level. In order to make the advertisement's message more intelligible, the above-mentioned fragment employs monosyllabic verbs – *get, gives, feel,* and *goes.* It also includes many favourable adjectives such as *infallible, freshwear, transfer-proof, water-proof, innovative, lightweight,* and *ultra-stretchable.* Some of them may be also clas- sified as compounds – *freshwear, transfer-proof, water-proof,* and *lightweight.* Furthermore, the *ultra-stretchable* adjective should be indicated as a coin- age neologism due to its affix *ultra-.* This group of adjectives add innovative and dynamic qualities to the advertisement through their vivid constructions. However, this advertisement not only encourages the recipient by employing a plethora of adjectives but also shortens the distance by using personal pronouns such as *you, your, our.*

On the rhetorical level, personification appears in a sentence: *Life doesn't compromise, so now your makeup doesn't either.* Its primary aim is to create a greater desire for the purchase by fostering more trust and affection in potential recipients. This sentence also makes use of parallelism as it does have the same structural form.

b. Advertisement made by ChatGPT 3.5
Prompt: *Please write a short description for the product L'oreal Foundation "Infallible 32H Freshwear Foundation in 20 Ivory, with vitamin C and SPF25" for the website advertisement. Please select and use some linguistic measures from semantic/syntactic/rhetorical level. Below the description, please indicate what types of linguistic measures you used and what is their objective in this advertisement.*

BOX 5.2   L'ORÉAL PARIS, FOUNDATION – ADVERTISEMENT BY CHATGPT 3.5

Discover L'oreal Infallible 32H Freshwear Foundation in 20 Ivory
Experience flawless beauty that lasts all day with L'oreal's Infallible 32H Freshwear Foundation in 20 Ivory. Enriched with vitamin C and boasting SPF25 protection, this lightweight formula effortlessly blends for a natural, matte finish that stays fresh for up to 32 hours. Whether you're facing a busy day or a special occasion, trust this foundation to keep your skin looking radiant and protected.

Linguistic measures used:

1. Favourable words (adjectives): "Flawless", "lasting", "natural", "matte", "radiant", "protected" – These adjectives aim to highlight the positive attributes of the foundation and evoke a sense of quality and desirability.
2. Superlative degree: "32H Freshwear" – The use of superlative suggests high performance and durability, enhancing the perceived value of the product.
3. Personal pronouns: "Your skin" – Directly addresses the consumer, creating a personal connection and implying the benefits are tailored to their needs.

4. Metaphor: "Radiant and protected" – Metaphorically connects the foundation's benefits (radiance and SPF protection) to desirable outcomes, enhancing its appeal.

Objectives in advertisement:

- Persuasion: By using favourable words and the superlative degree, the advertisement aims to persuade consumers of the foundation's superior quality and long-lasting benefits.
- Engagement: Personal pronouns engage the reader directly, making them feel the benefits are specifically for them.
- Memorability: Metaphorical language enhances the memorability of the benefits, making the product more memorable and enticing to potential buyers.

The L'Oréal Paris foundation advertisement proposed by ChatGPT 3.5 is correctly executed, although some shortcomings are noticeable. Though it missed a few, ChatGPT did a decent job of identifying the linguistic measures it employed.

Most remarkably, it only included measures at the lexical and rhetorical levels, even though the advertisement's first opening sentence belongs to a syntactic level that is not listed. With only nine words, the short sentence *Discover L'oreal Infallible 32H Freshwear Foundation in 20 Ivory* is easy to read and retain. It also fits the definition of a simple sentence since it lacks complicated grammatical constructions.

According to the lexical level, chat has provided a sufficient list of favourable adjectives; however, it omitted two that ought to appear on this list – *fresh* and *lightweight*. Furthermore, the words *lightweight* and *freshwear* also function as a compound, but again, not listed by ChatGPT. Advertisement created by AI also provides the usage of personal pronouns such as *your* skin and *you*'re. Once more, though, there was no mention of *you* in the list provided. Subsequently, *32H Freshwear* is not an adjective, hence it cannot serve as a superlative, despite ChatGPT 3.5's indication of being a superlative degree. Additionally, monosyllabic verbs like *last, blends, stays, trust,* and *keep* were used by chat but were not indicated. Furthermore, the advertisement used weasel words like *enriched* and *up to*, none of which were mentioned; however, they can convert highly persuasive messages leading to purchasing a product.

At the rhetorical level, ChatGPT used only one linguistic measure – the metaphor of *radiant and protected* skin. Although this particular metaphor definitely evokes positive emotions and vivid images in consumers, it probably does not influence memorability that much as highlighted by AI.

Despite the previously noted limitations, ChatGPT 3.5 successfully composed the product advertisement. The model effectively articulated the objectives and utilised various linguistic strategies to achieve them. Nonetheless, it failed to enumerate all the employed linguistic measures and could not categorise them at all.

c. Advertisement made by ChatGPT 4.0

**BOX 5.3   L'ORÉAL PARIS, FOUNDATION –
ADVERTISEMENT BY CHATGPT 4.0**

Experience unstoppable beauty with L'Oréal's Infallible 32H Freshwear Foundation in 20 Ivory. This foundation is not just a cover-up; it's your skin's new best friend. Enriched with Vitamin C and fortified with SPF 25, it ensures your skin looks flawless and feels vibrant all day and night. Dive into a world of long-lasting perfection where fine lines fade and radiance emerges. Choose Infallible, because you're worth it.

Linguistic measures used:

1. Favourable adjectives (lexical level): Using words like "unstoppable", "flawless", and "radiant" enhances the product's appeal by attributing positive qualities to it. This strategy aims to create an emotional connection with the customer, suggesting that using the product will lead to a highly desirable outcome.
2. Personal pronouns (lexical level): The pronoun "your" personalizes the message, making it seem as though the advertisement speaks directly to the reader. This approach helps narrow the gap between the brand and the consumer, making the advertisement more relatable and effective.
3. Imperative sentences (syntactic level): The command "Choose Infallible" serves as a direct call to action. Imperatives are used to influence consumer behaviour, encouraging them to make a purchase decision.
4. Minor sentences (syntactic level): The phrase "because you're worth it" is a minor sentence that lacks a formal subject and verb, creating a memorable and impactful slogan that resonates emotionally with the audience.

5. Hyperbole (rhetorical level): Describing the foundation as "Infallible" exaggerates its effectiveness, implying that it cannot fail to meet the user's expectations. This exaggeration aims to emphasise the product's reliability and high quality.

Compared to its previous version, ChatGPT 4.0 performed noticeably better when creating the L'oreal foundation advertisement. It produced an extremely convincing advertising message and performed an outstanding task of presenting the promoted product. Nonetheless, it is important to note that, like its earlier version, it did not encompass every linguistic measure utilised. However, it effectively categorised the measures into lexical, syntactic, and rhetorical levels and clearly articulated their purposes.

The measures that were not mentioned by AI, again, were related to lexical level. Monosyllabic verbs like looks, feels, choose, and compounds like cover-up and long-lasting were used but they were not included on the list. Also, weasel words like *experience, enriched, ensures*, and *dive into* were used by ChatGPT 4.0. AI-generated advertisements also come up with the use of pronouns like *your* and *you*. Again, the word *you* was not mentioned in the provided list of linguistic measures.

Despite that, the most recent version of ChatGPT performed a great job of enumerating and classifying linguistic measures at the syntactic level. The minor sentence with the phrase *Because you're worth it* is one of the most significant measures it employs in this advertisement. The brand makes use of this slogan numerous times and in this way everyone associates them with this phrase. Also, apart from being brisk and rhythmic, it strongly affects the product's memorability and is closely linked to the brand.

Regretfully, ChatGPT 4.0 classified the rhetorical measures given data entirely incorrectly in the list even though it employed. The fact that the word *infallible* is considered to be a favourable adjective rather than a hyperbole indicates that the AI mismatched the term. It also did not list other sophisticated rhetorical measures it employed instead. The first is the personification of *your skin's new best friend*, which may encourage customers to feel greater trust in the product. Another is the metaphor with the sentence *dive into the world of long-lasting perfection*, which thanks to the compound word *long-lasting* creates a strongly persuasive message. Concerning the rhetorical measures used, the consumer may imagine that when along with the advertised foundation, they can create an amazing look on their face that will last as long as desired.

Example 2

a. Advertisement made by a human

> **BOX 5.4   AVON, MASCARA – ADVERTISEMENT BY A HUMAN**
>
> *When it comes to length with volume, does your mascara measure up? Our Legendary Lengths Mascara gives you guaranteed satisfaction, because when it comes to your lashes #SizeMatters. Shop today for increased length and volume!*

In the above-mentioned fragment, Avon focuses mainly on the syntactic level of linguistic features. Their advertisement contains two significant sentences, appropriately interrogative and imperative.

1. *When it comes to length with volume, does your mascara measure up?*
2. *Shop today for increased length and volume!*

The first sentence creates a presupposition effect by implying indirectly that their mascara has a high quality. As it often happens, the advertiser additionally answers the question themselves in the sentence that follows – *Our Legendary Lengths Mascara gives you guaranteed satisfaction, because when it comes to your lashes #SizeMatters.* The second, imperative sentence has also a strong persuasive effect since it is urging the consumer to take the action and buy the product. It also involves a weasel word in a phrase <u>*gives*</u> *you guaranteed satisfaction*. Indeed, it suggests a highly positive meaning, but in fact, it does not make any real guarantee.

This advertisement should be called well-thought-out as it is written in plain language. That statement can be evidenced by lexical aspects such as monosyllabic verbs (*comes, gives, shop*) and personal pronouns (*you, your, our*). Moreover, it contains one hyperbole and alliteration when it comes to rhetorical level – <u>*L*</u>*egendary* <u>*L*</u>*engths Mascara*. By introducing the phrase *legendary lengths*, the advertiser suggests that their product can make lashes unimaginably long and also repeats the letter *L* for a soothing effect.

b. Advertisement made by ChatGPT 3.5
Prompt: *Please write a short description for the website advertisement for the mascara Avon "Legendary Lengths Mascara" which gives length and volume.*

Please select and use some linguistic measures from semantic/syntactic/rhetorical level. Below the description, please indicate what types of linguistic measures you used and what is their objective in this advertisement.

BOX 5.5   AVON, MASCARA – ADVERTISEMENT BY CHATGPT 3.5

Introducing Avon Legendary Lengths Mascara
Transform your lashes with Avon's Legendary Lengths Mascara, your secret to captivating length and voluminous lashes. This innovative formula delivers unparalleled definition and thickness, effortlessly enhancing your natural beauty. Whether you're going for a subtle daytime look or glamorous evening allure, Avon's mascara ensures your lashes command attention wherever you go.

Linguistic measures used:

1. Favourable words (adjectives): "Captivating", "legendary", "voluminous", "innovative", "effortlessly", "enhancing", "command attention" – These adjectives aim to evoke positive emotions and associations with the product, emphasising its effectiveness and desirability.
2. Metaphor: "Your secret to captivating length and voluminous lashes" – The metaphorical use of "secret" implies exclusivity and special benefits, suggesting that using this mascara will unlock desirable outcomes for the user.
3. Imperative sentences: "Transform your lashes", "Ensure your lashes command attention" – Imperative sentences give commands or instructions, encouraging the reader to take action and try the product, thereby enhancing engagement and persuasiveness.

Objectives in advertisement:

- Persuasion: The use of favourable words and metaphorical language persuades consumers of the mascara's ability to enhance lashes dramatically, making them appear longer and fuller.
- Engagement: Imperative sentences directly engage the reader, prompting them to envision themselves using the product and achieving the advertised benefits.

- Desirability: By using captivating adjectives and metaphor, the advertisement creates a sense of desirability and allure around the product, making it more appealing to potential buyers.

The Avon mascara advertisement generated by ChatGPT 3.5, in comparison to previous advertisements, lacks monosyllabic verbs. Despite its rich vocabulary, featuring favourable adjectives such as *captivating, voluminous, innovative*, and *enhancing*, this absence may render the advertisement incomprehensible and burdensome for some consumers. Additionally, the phrase previously made by a human – *legendary lengths*, serving as both alliteration and hyperbole – was omitted in identification by ChatGPT.

Personal pronouns (*you* and *your*) were not included in the summary list of used linguistic measures made by ChatGPT, although they are present in the advertisement. The same with weasel words such as *transform, delivers,* and *ensures*. Furthermore, the ChatGPT once again did not categorise the linguistic devices used according to their levels, and also there were errors in its identification. Firstly, the AI incorrectly identified *your secret to captivating length and voluminous lashes* as a metaphor, which it is not. Secondly, it mistakenly classified *command attention* as an adjective, which is also inaccurate.

Overall, ChatGPT 3.5 demonstrated moderate effectiveness in generating an advertisement for Avon brand mascara. Although it established appropriate objectives and utilised relevant linguistic measures, the resulting advertisement was too highbrow. Additionally, the identification list produced by ChatGPT lacked accuracy and reliability.

c. Advertisement made by ChatGPT 4.0

BOX 5.6   AVON, MASCARA – ADVERTISEMENT BY CHATGPT 4.0

Unleash the legend within with Avon's Legendary Lengths Mascara. Elevate your look to epic proportions as each stroke delivers unparalleled length and voluminous curves. Crafted to captivate, this mascara promises to transform your lashes from simple to spectacular. Make every blink a statement. Discover the power of your most mesmerizing gaze yet.

Linguistic measures used:

1. Neologisms (lexical level): The phrase "Legendary Lengths" uses a compound as a form of neologism, combining familiar words to create a new, memorable product name that highlights its unique selling proposition of enhancing lash length.
2. Imperative sentences (syntactic level): The command "Unleash the legend within" and "Make every blink a statement" are imperative sentences that actively engage the reader, prompting immediate interest and encouraging them to imagine the transformative potential of the mascara.
3. Hyperbole (rhetorical level): Phrases like "unparalleled length" and "voluminous curves" are examples of hyperbole, exaggerating the effects of the mascara to attract consumers by promising exceptional results.
4. Alliteration (rhetorical level): The use of alliteration in "Legendary Lengths" and "lashes from simple to spectacular" makes the description more rhythmic and memorable, enhancing the overall appeal of the message and making it more pleasing to read.
5. Metaphor (rhetorical level): Describing the mascara as "crafted to captivate" employs a metaphor, suggesting that the product not only beautifies but also holds a captivating power akin to a finely crafted artefact. This enriches the description by implying that the product is meticulously made to achieve the best results.

The advertising proposed by ChatGPT 4.0 is far superior to that proposed by version 3.5 but it, like the previous one, has some shortcomings. ChatGPT 4.0 uses a variety of linguistic measures, but only 40% of those listed were recognised accurately.

The linguistic measures used in this advertisement, which AI correctly recognises, mainly involve imperative sentences. The advertisement excels at the syntactical level. As many as four out of five sentences are imperative (only the third sentence is not), serving as a motivation for consumers to take action and purchase the product. Other correctly identified linguistic measures are alliteration in *legendary lengths* (previously written by a human) and *lashes from simple to spectacular*. However, the use of the *s* sound in advertisements should be omitted, thus it can be a symbol of danger or lead the consumers to believe they are being tricked.

In addition to these linguistic measures, Chat suggested a few more, which he was unable to identify. Again, the personal pronoun *your* was used. It also used a lot of favourable adjectives, such as *legendary, epic, unparalleled, voluminous*, *spectacular*, and *mesmerising*, which certainly reinforces the product's attractiveness.

As for some anomalies, the first point on the list refers to a neologism that stands for *legendary lengths*. Unfortunately, *legendary lengths* is not a newly invented word, meaning it is not a neologism and was incorrectly identified. Metaphor is another example of an incorrectly identified point. The list ended with the phrase *crafted to captivate*, which was not a metaphor. Hyperbole is present in ChatGPT's advertisement (*unparalleled lengths* and *voluminous curves*), although one was not identified by Chat (*epic proportions*).

Although the objectives were correctly stated and the advertisement was written constructively, using a variety of linguistic means at all levels, it is observable that ChatGPT, whether in version 4.0 or 3.5, has difficulty in identifying correctly the measures used.

Example 3

a. Advertisement made by a human

BOX 5.7   THEBALMJOUR, LIP STAIN – ADVERTISEMENT BY A HUMAN

Lip stains to up your gloss game for a perfect mix of stain and shine! With a uniquely flexible formula, theBalmJour starts as a gloss, finishes as a stain, and delivers the high-pigment payoff of a lipstick. And since these creamy, moisturizing lip stains have serious staying power, you'll never have to say, "adieu".

The Balm advertisement targets the lexical and rhetorical levels. When it comes to rhetoric, the advertiser applied the punning in the word *theBalmJour* which probably refers to the French word *bonjour* meaning *hello* in English. Due to the punning, the advertisements make the product amusing and noticeable.

In terms of lexical level and French references, the advertiser applies the borrowed word *adieu* meaning *goodbye*. This measure makes the product appear more exotic and intriguing. Moreover, there are some favourable adjectives such *as perfect, flexible, creamy, moisturizing, staying,* and *high-pigment*. Thus, they empower consumers in developing a positive attitude towards the product. The last one, *high-pigment*, is also a coinage neologism, which implies that the lip stain has extraordinary qualities (in this example – the pigment). The advertiser did not omit the application of a weasel word – <u>to</u> <u>up</u> *your gloss game*. Again, with an attempt and worthless promise to help us with their product. By using personal pronouns such as *you* and *your*, the commercial relates to us directly making the message more relevant.

b. Advertisement made by ChatGPT 3.5
Prompt: *Please write a short description for the website advertisement for the theBalmJour creamy lip stain. Please select and use some linguistic measures from semantic/syntactic/rhetorical level. Below the description, please indicate what types of linguistic measures you used and what is their objective in this advertisement.*

BOX 5.8   THEBALMJOUR, LIP STAIN – ADVERTISEMENT BY CHATGPT 3.5

Discover theBalmJour Creamy Lip Stain
Elevate your lip game with theBalmJour Creamy Lip Stain, where vibrant color meets lasting comfort. This luxurious lip stain combines the richness of a lipstick with the lightweight feel of a lip stain, ensuring a flawless, velvety finish that lasts for hours. Infused with nourishing ingredients like shea butter and vitamin E, it keeps your lips hydrated and supple throughout the day. Available in a spectrum of shades from subtle nudes to bold reds, theBalmJour is your go-to for effortless elegance and all-day wear.

Linguistic measures used:

1. Favourable words (adjectives): "Vibrant", "lasting", "luxurious", "flawless", "velvety", "nourishing", "effortless", "all-day" – These adjectives aim to highlight the positive attributes and benefits of the product, enhancing its appeal and desirability.
2. Metaphor: "Combines the richness of a lipstick with the lightweight feel of a lip stain" – This metaphorical expression creates a vivid image of the product's dual benefits, emphasising its unique selling proposition and appeal to potential buyers.
3. Parallelism: "Effortless elegance and all-day wear" – The parallel structure reinforces the benefits of the product in a concise and memorable way, appealing to consumers looking for both style and longevity in their lip products.

Objectives in advertisement:

- Desirability: The use of favourable adjectives and metaphorical language aims to make the product appealing and desirable, highlighting its luxurious qualities and long-lasting benefits.
- Differentiation: By comparing the product to both lipstick and lip stain with the metaphor, the advertisement distinguishes theBalm-Jour as a unique hybrid that offers the best of both worlds.
- Credibility: Mentioning nourishing ingredients like shea butter and vitamin E builds credibility and assures potential customers of the product's quality and its beneficial effects on lip health.

The Balm's Lip Stain advertisement written by ChatGPT 3.5 has linguistic measures at the lexical and syntactic levels, as well as at the rhetorical level. Nevertheless, as it turns out, Chat correctly identified them only at the lexical and rhetorical levels, although the identification of several linguistic measures still lacking.

The vast number of favourable adjectives positively influence the advertising message, which becomes very persuasive as a result of their use. In addition to the eight mentioned by ChatGPT, i.e. *vibrant, lasting, flawless, velvety, nourishing, effortless, all-day,* there was one more, i.e. *lightweight.* The adjectives *lightweight* and *all-day* are also compounds, further enhancing the positive perception and making the consumer feel intrigued. Moreover, it makes the advertisement more appealing.

Furthermore, on the lexical level, the personal pronoun *your* appears, which is another clever use of ChatGPT 3.5, whereby the distance between the advertising product and the consumer is reduced. Weasel words, i.e., *the feel of* and *ensuring* also fall into this category. As such, the advertisement can manipulate the consumer because it assures about something which, in the case of an individual, is not necessarily real after all.

On the syntactic level, two measures have emerged. The first one a short, simple sentence – *Discover theBalmJour Creamy Lip Stain*, which at the same time can be imperative, as can the second one in the sentence *Elevate your lip game with theBalmJour Lip Stain.* Unfortunately, none of the above were identified by ChatGPT.

One parallel structure appeared on the rhetorical level. Also, it correctly identified and posited the objective of its use. By contrast, the metaphor was misidentified, as the statement *combines the richness of a lipstick with the lightweight feel of a lip stain* is certainly not metaphorical in any sense. It is disappointing that Chat failed to spot the punning in the word theBalmJour, which is also the name of the product and was already discussed in the ad written by the man.

All things considered, the advertisement is nicely done and, apart from a few minor flaws, there is nothing to be complained about. Favourable adjectives are at the forefront and stand out strongly in this advertisement as the main used linguistic measures.

c. Advertisement made by ChatGPT 4.0

BOX 5.9   THEBALMJOUR, LIP STAIN – ADVERTISEMENT BY CHATGPT 4.0

Welcome a new era of lip color with theBalmJour creamy lip stain. A perfect fusion of enduring color and unparalleled comfort, this lip stain glides on with creamy ease, setting into a stunning matte finish that lasts all day. From morning meetings to evening soirées, maintain flawless, vibrant lips that speak volumes without saying a word. Embrace the journey to beautiful lips with theBalmJour.

Linguistic measures used:

1. Personification (rhetorical level): By suggesting the lips "speak volumes without saying a word", personification is used to give life and agency to the lips. This rhetorical device creates a visual and emotional impact, emphasising how the lip stain enhances more than just appearance – it enhances expression.
2. Positive adjectives (lexical level): Adjectives like "enduring", "unparalleled", "creamy", "stunning", and "flawless" positively describe the product's attributes, building a strong appeal by highlighting its quality and benefits.
3. Imperative sentences (syntactic level): The phrase "Embrace the journey to beautiful lips" is an imperative sentence, providing a direct call to action that encourages consumers to try the product and anticipate its transformative potential.
4. Neologisms (lexical level): The product name "theBalmJour" itself is a neologism, blending "balm" and a playful take on "bonjour" to suggest a greeting to a new style or product experience, making it catchy and memorable.
5. Alliteration (rhetorical level): The alliteration in "perfect fusion of enduring color and unparalleled comfort" uses the repetition of the "c" sound to make the description smooth and pleasing to read, enhancing the lyrical quality of the advertisement.

Advertisement written by ChatGPT 4.0 makes excellent use of language measures at all levels. Language measures, i.e., positive adjectives, imperative sentences, and neologisms were correctly identified and matched to appropriate linguistic levels at 60%.

ChatGPT failed to identify alliteration since, in alliteration, repeated sounds occur in sequence, which is not the case for the phrase *perfect fusion of enduring colour and unparalleled comfort*. Furthermore, Chat incorrectly matched the phrase *speak volumes without saying a word*. It is assumed that it is a personification, although it is not. In fact, the idiom *to speak volumes* is not only used in the sense of a person, but also to a thing, and thus cannot connect with personification.[1] Possibly a better choice would be to use it in a mascara advertisement, which would make an appealing wordplay, as it is the volume that is sought in mascara. Despite the misidentification, it is an eye-catching phrase.

An intriguing language measure that was not included in the summary list provided by AI is the word *soirees*. In accordance with the dictionary, a *soiree* is a social gathering held in the evening.[2] It is a kind of neologism of a so-called borrowed word, which makes the product seem more exotic and hence more intriguing. The neologism was used probably for the sake of the product name *theBalmjour*, which refers to the French greeting *bonjour*. In this way, the advertisement became very coherent.

What is surprising is that no personal pronouns have been used in the advertisement, making it seem distant and not directly aimed at the consumer. Nevertheless, it is very well-written, and what perfectly encapsulates it is the final sentence *Embrace the journey to beautiful lips with theBalmJour*, which, apart from being imperative, is also simple and short, so it is bound to be more easily remembered and it prompts action. Who would not want to experience such an adventure?

Example 4

a. Advertisement made by a human

**BOX 5.10   THE BALM COSMETICS, CONCEALER –
ADVERTISEMENT BY A HUMAN**

Anne T. Dotes Concealer is a clean, stealth, skin perfectionist. Finally making her debut, this adorable, 100% recyclable tin makes this little lady extremely desirable. Not to mention, her ability to conceal redness, discoloration, and under-eye circles is un'can'ny. Loaded with

> *good-for-your-skin ingredients like Organic Jojoba and Sunflower Oils, this remedy is always at your fingertips ready to assist. Available in 10 gorgeous shades.*

The Balm advertisement will be analysed again, as this time it has undertaken linguistic features at all three levels and is especially interesting in terms of a rhetorical level. Correspondingly, on a rhetorical level, the advertisement makes use of punning and personification. *Anne T. Dotes* is a pun since it sounds like antidotes and an antidote is "something that corrects or counteracts something undesirable".[3] This word play used by the advertiser is extremely efficient. What is more, the pun also refers to the personification as *Anne T. Dotes* is the name of a *little lady* who is in fact a concealer.

On the lexical level, there is also a reference to a *little lady* as the advertisement uses personal pronouns like *her* and *your*. It tries to create a bond between us – a consumer and her – a *little lady* who is attempting to help us. The commercial is rich in adjectives – *clean, stealth, adorable, recyclable, desirable, under-eye, uncanny, good-for-your-skin, gorgeous*. Their appearance convey a positive attitude towards the described product. *Under-eye* and *good-for-your-skin* are also compounds which attract attention of the consumer.

By means of syntactic level, the first (*Anne T. Dotes Concealer is a clean, stealth, skin perfectionist*) and the last (*Available in 10 gorgeous shades*) sentences are short and simple. Despite the complexity of the advertisement in other sentences, these two perfectly open and close it, thus facilitating a persuasive message. It can be overall concluded that the advertisement has been well thought out and is highly persuasive and manipulative.

b. Advertisement made by ChatGPT 3.5
Prompt: *Please write a short description for the website advertisement for the Anne T. Dotes Concealer available in 10 shades, 100% recyclable. Please select and use some linguistic measures from semantic/syntactic/rhetorical level. Below the description, please indicate what types of linguistic measures you used and what is their objective in this advertisement.*

BOX 5.11   THE BALM COSMETICS, CONCEALER – ADVERTISEMENT BY CHATGPT 3.5

Discover Anne T. Dotes Concealer: Your Perfect Match in 10 Shades
   Achieve flawless complexion effortlessly with Anne T. Dotes Concealer, crafted in 10 versatile shades to suit every skin tone. This eco-conscious beauty essential not only covers imperfections seamlessly but also supports sustainability with its 100% recyclable packaging. Elevate your beauty routine with a product that cares for your skin and the planet.

Linguistic measures used:

1. Semantic level:
   - Positive adjectives: "flawless", "versatile", "seamlessly", "eco-conscious", "sustainability", "recyclable", "supports", "cares".
   - Neologism (coinage): "Anne T. Dotes" (a play on "anecdotes", creating a memorable brand name).
2. Syntactic level:
   - Simple sentences: Easy-to-read sentences to enhance readability and convey clear benefits.
   - Imperative sentence: "Discover Anne T. Dotes Concealer" encourages immediate action from the reader.
3. Rhetorical level:
   - Metaphor: "Achieve flawless complexion effortlessly" compares using the concealer to achieving perfection effortlessly.
   - Alliteration: "Crafted in 10 versatile shades" adds a rhythmic quality and emphasises the variety of shades available.

Objectives:

- Variety and inclusivity: By highlighting the concealer's availability in ten shades, the advertisement aims to appeal to a diverse audience of consumers with different skin tones, ensuring inclusivity and catering to individual preferences.
- Environmental responsibility: Emphasising the 100% recyclable packaging aims to attract environmentally-conscious consumers who prioritise eco-friendly products, thereby promoting sustainable beauty choices and reducing environmental impact.
- Ease of use and convenience: By emphasising the seamless coverage and effortless application, the advertisement aims to position

the concealer as a convenient and effective solution for achieving flawless skin, appealing to consumers looking for easy-to-use beauty products.
- Brand trust and credibility: Mentioning the brand name "Anne T. Dotes" and highlighting its commitment to quality and consumer satisfaction aims to build brand trust and credibility, encouraging potential customers to choose this concealer over competitors.

While the advertisement itself is not written in a wrong manner and has correctly posed objectives, it has a completely misguided and incorrect identification of language measures.

On the lexical level, the most striking one is the alleged neologism *Anne T. Dotes*, which ChatGPT explains as a *play on anecdotes*. This is not a neologism but a pun on the word *antidote*. Besides, there were two verbs in the positive adjectives listed – *supports* and *cares*. In addition, there was one weasel word used in the phrase *to suit every skin tone*, which is misleading to the consumer, as the concealer does not necessarily have to suit all skin tones.

As far as the syntactic level is concerned, unfortunately, the sentences are not "easy-to-read" at all due to their complexity. The complexity is also indicated by the absence of monosyllabic verbs. The overly advanced vocabulary used makes the advertisement no longer versatile, and some individuals may find it difficult to understand and perceive it properly. The rhetorical level has also been misrepresented. The metaphor and alliteration have been absolutely misidentified.

In conclusion, this is a rather badly composed advertisement in terms of language, although its objectives have been aptly presented.

c. Advertisement made by ChatGPT 4.0

BOX 5.12   THE BALM COSMETICS, CONCEALER – ADVERTISEMENT BY CHATGPT 4.0

Discover the secret to flawless skin with Anne T. Dotes Concealer, your eco-conscious beauty ally. Available in 10 stunning shades, this concealer promises perfect coverage for all skin tones. Embrace a blend of beauty and responsibility with our 100% recyclable packaging, reflecting your commitment to the planet. Anne T. Dotes: because true beauty is more than skin deep.

Linguistic measures used:

1. Pun (rhetorical level): The product name "Anne T. Dotes" is a pun on "antidotes", suggesting that the concealer is a remedy for skin imperfections. This playful wordplay engages the reader and underscores the effectiveness of the product.
2. Parallelism (rhetorical level): The phrase "a blend of beauty and responsibility" uses parallel structure to equally emphasise both the aesthetic and ethical appeals of the product. This rhetorical device enhances the message's persuasiveness by showing that the product satisfies multiple values simultaneously.
3. Comparative adjectives (lexical level): Using the adjective "stunning" to describe the shades available enhances the appeal by suggesting high-quality and visually impressive results. This choice of adjective elevates the perceived value of the product.
4. Imperative sentence (syntactic level): The call to action "Embrace a blend of beauty and responsibility" is an imperative sentence, directly engaging the consumer to take action not just by purchasing but by making a choice that aligns with broader values.
5. Alliteration (rhetorical level): The use of alliteration in "perfect coverage for all" creates a pleasing auditory effect that makes the text more memorable and engaging to the reader.

The version of the advertisement presented by ChatGPT 4.0 is better in every aspect. The first thing that stands out is the properly detected pun, which ChatGPT 3.5 struggled with. ChatGPT 4.0 concludes that "product name *Anne T. Dotes* is a pun on *antidotes*, suggesting that the concealer is a remedy for skin imperfection", which is a great identification and representation of the objective.

In addition, personal pronouns were used in the advertisement, and this time AI did not only use *your*, as the word *our* also appeared in this advertisement. This is meaningful as *your-our* creates an involuntary bond between the consumer and the advertiser. Unfortunately, this has not been identified although it plays a key role.

In terms of mistakes, there are three. Firstly, parallelism has been misidentified. Secondly, the *comparative* adjectives should be called *favourable* adjectives, i.e. *flawless, eco-consious, perfect*, and *recyclable* should be added to the list. Incidentally, it is worth adding that *eco-consious* is also a compound. Thirdly, the phrase "perfect coverage for all" cannot be considered alliteration.

Moreover, it is worth mentioning that the last sentence *Anne T. Dotes: because true beauty is more than skin deep* is essential in that advertisement. Although it is a complex sentence, it makes a great slogan that will be definitely remembered by the consumer.

In conclusion, this advertisement is well constructed. The main merit of that is the correctly detected punning as well as the use of personal pronouns and favourable adjectives. However, its greatest merit is the slogan in the last sentence, which is highly persuasive and will be associated with the brand's particular product.

Example 5

a. Advertisement made by a human

**BOX 5.13   THE BALM COSMETICS, HIGHLIGHTER –
ADVERTISEMENT BY A HUMAN**

This highlighter, shimmer and shadow illuminates skin with an ultra-soft gold radiance that is buildable from light to bright without ever looking glittery or shiny. Let's Bolt is formulated with high power botanicals that boost the skin's natural radiance and are completely void of bad guy ingredients like Talc, Synthetic Binders, PTFE and Parabens. Apply on your cheeks, nose, and eyelids for a dazzling glow that's out of this world!

The above-mentioned advertisement is manifested on all linguistic levels. First of all, it employs some adjectives like *ultra-soft, buildable, high power, natural,* and *dazzling.* Each of them has a favourable meaning and arouses a desire for the product. *Ultra-soft* is also a coinage neologism that implies the product has an unusual soft radiance. Words "are" and "have" "have always been an important part of efficient marketing.

On the rhetorical level, two features appear – hyperbole and personification. The phrase *bad guy ingredients* is a personification that gives the ingredients human characteristics. In this way, it leads to various associations and attracts more consumers. *A dazzling glow that's out of this world* connects with the hyperbole that is dramatising the selling point. It implies that the consumer can gain superhuman benefits, in this case – glow, from a product.

Last but not least, the sentence – *Apply on your cheeks, nose, and eyelids for a dazzling glow that's out of this world!* – is imperative and refers to the syntactic level. It gives a command or instruction which is preferred in encouraging the consumer to gain and use the product.

b. Advertisement made by ChatGPT 3.5

Prompt: *Please write a short description for the website advertisement for the Balm Comestics highlighter "Let's Bolt" which is void of bad guy ingredients like Talc, Synthetic Binders, PTFE and Parabens. Please select and use some linguistic measures from semantic/syntactic/rhetorical level. Below the description, please indicate what types of linguistic measures you used and what is their objective in this advertisement.*

BOX 5.14   THE BALM COSMETICS, HIGHLIGHTER –
ADVERTISEMENT BY CHATGPT 3.5

Illuminate Your Beauty with theBalm Cosmetics "Let's Bolt" Highlighter
*   Discover the radiance of theBalm Cosmetics "Let's Bolt" Highlighter, crafted without harmful ingredients such as Talc, Synthetic Binders, PTFE, and Parabens. This luxurious highlighter delivers a natural glow that enhances your features while caring for your skin. Its finely milled formula ensures seamless application and long-lasting luminosity, perfect for creating a dewy, illuminated complexion. Choose "Let's Bolt" for a guilt-free glow that celebrates beauty without compromise.*

Linguistic measures used:

1. Exclusion of harmful ingredients: "Void of bad guy ingredients like Talc, Synthetic Binders, PTFE, and Parabens" – This emphasises the product's clean and safe formulation, appealing to consumers who prioritise skincare and avoid potentially harmful additives.

2. Positive adjectives: "Radiance", "luxurious", "seamless", "long-lasting luminosity" – These adjectives evoke a sense of luxury, quality, and effectiveness, portraying the highlighter as a high-performance beauty product.

3. Ethical appeal: The phrase "guilt-free glow" appeals to ethical consumers who seek products that align with their values of clean beauty and skincare safety.

Objectives in advertisement:

• Safety and clean beauty: By highlighting the absence of harmful ingredients, the advertisement aims to attract consumers who prioritise clean beauty products and are cautious about what they apply to their skin.

- Quality and performance: The use of positive adjectives and descriptions of the highlighter's benefits aim to convince consumers of its effectiveness in delivering a natural, long-lasting glow.
- Ethical and value-based appeal: The emphasis on "guilt-free glow" appeals to consumers who value ethical consumption and seek products that align with their personal values of health and sustainability.

In this advertisement, ChatGPT 3.5 only recognised one linguistic measure (the other two are not even language measures), although it used more than one. The correctly recognised and used language measure is positive adjectives, its objective is also accurate. The first of the incorrectly discerned ones is *exclusion of harmful ingredients*, which is a good accurate point but it is not a linguistic measure. The second, on the other hand, is *ethical appeal*. In this case, it is not a linguistic measure and also a wrong choice of the objective. The adjective *guilt-free* in the phrase *guilt-free glow* is related to stunning glow and is not connected to ethical values.

The language measures used that were not detected are the personal pronoun – *your*, the simple and imperative sentence – *Illuminate your beauty [...]*, the compound – *long-lasting*, and the alliteration – *long-lasting luminosity*, which gives a soothing effect of sounds. This shows that linguistic measures were found at every linguistic level.

The advertisement, despite the well-positioned objectives of *safety and clean beauty*, and *quality and performance,* is rather over-complicated by the predominance of complex sentences and long difficult words. Furthermore, ChatGPT 3.5 only managed 33% with the identification list of what types of linguistic measures it used.

c. Advertisement made by ChatGPT 4.0

BOX 5.15   THE BALM COSMETICS, HIGHLIGHTER – ADVERTISEMENT BY CHATGPT 4.0

Illuminate your complexion with The Balm Cosmetics' "Let's Bolt" highlighter, where purity meets luminosity. Free from talc, synthetic binders, PTFE, and parabens, this highlighter is your guilt-free gateway to glowing skin. Crafted for brilliance, "Let's Bolt" ensures you shine without compromise. Light up your features with a sweep of clean, clear, and radiant glow that speaks volumes about your beauty ethics.

Linguistic measures used:

1. Metaphor (rhetorical level): The phrase "gateway to glowing skin" is a metaphor that enriches the description by implying that using this product is an entry into a new state of beauty and health. This evokes a transformative experience for the user.
2. Euphemism (lexical level): The description "free from" instead of "does not contain" softens the message and creates a positive framing, which reassures the consumer about what the product lacks without focusing on the absence of these ingredients.
3. Imperative sentence (syntactic level): The command "Light up your features" uses an imperative sentence to directly engage the consumer and encourage them to use the product to enhance their appearance.
4. Alliteration (rhetorical level): In "clean, clear, and radiant glow", the repeated "c" sound creates a melodious and memorable phrase, enhancing the text's appeal and making the benefits more impactful.
5. Personification (rhetorical level): The phrase "ensures you shine without compromise" personifies the highlighter, giving it the agency to guarantee an outcome. This suggests reliability and effectiveness, building trust in the product.

The advertisement proposed by ChatGPT 4.0 is generally well-made although what is missing is a proper listing of the linguistic measures used and their objectives. However, those that AI listed were correctly matched to the appropriate levels, in this case rhetorical.

Correctly listed by ChatGPT 4.0 is a metaphor along with the phrase *gateway to glowing skin*. This is a great advantage because, judging by previous advertisements, Chat mostly encounters difficulties in creating and identifying metaphors correctly. In addition, there was also the alliteration *"clean, clear"*, which was identified, and the sound "c" with its way of affecting the consumer was explained. The AI failed to successfully identify the euphemism, imperative sentence, and personification.

Among the more interesting linguistic measures, a rhyme appeared in the phrase *purity meets luminosity*, which creates a melodic overtone. In addition, favourable adjectives were used, i.e. *guilt-free* (which is also a compound), *glowing, clean, clear,* and *radiant.* Personal pronouns, i.e., *you* and *your* also appeared.

In a nutshell, language measures were used at the lexical level, which went completely undetected, and also at the rhetorical level, where ChatGPT correctly recognised metaphor and alliteration. By combining these two measures in an advertisement, the lack of use of syntactic-level linguistic measures is irrelevant.

2. Skin/body/hair care products

Example 1

a. Advertisement made by a human

**BOX 5.16   THE BODY SHOP, BODY YOGHURT –
ADVERTISEMENT BY A HUMAN**

Help keep skin feeling and smelling fresh all summer with our special edition Refreshing Passionfruit Body Yogurt. Jump in the shower. Jump out. Smooth on our Body Yogurt. Jump in your jeans. Get on with your summer. It won't last forever, right?

The above-mentioned commercial holds a variety of linguistic features and it includes them in all three levels. At the lexical level, it makes use of monosyllabic verbs such as *help, keep, jump,* and *get.* Again, their use refers to the selling power through a simple message. In the case of selling power, a weasel word was also introduced. *Help keep skin feeling and smelling fresh all summer* – it promises that the skin will feel and smell fresh. The advertiser gives us an illusion that they attempt to help us with their product rather than merely sell it. What is more, they employ personal pronouns – *our* and *your.* That clearly suggests a friendly one-to-one connection between the advertiser and the consumer.

When it comes to the syntactic level, the whole fragment is full of simple, short, minor, and imperative sentences such as *Jump in the shower, Jump out, Smooth on our Body Yogurt, Jump in your jeans,* and *Get on with your summer.* In these terms, a readability of the text increases and the advertisement is more affordable. Through the applied imperative forms, it also induces purchase. By employing minor sentences, the text can be considered informal – again, it connects the advertiser and the consumer. The last sentence in the fragment – *It won't last forever, right?* – is an interrogative sentence and gives a strong persuasive effect. It applies a *yes* answer since it is general knowledge that summer indeed "won't last forever".

On the matter of rhetorical level, the advertisement utilises one linguistic device – a parallelism. It facilitates faster absorption of the advertising message by frequently repeating the same structural grammatical pattern. *Jump in the shower. Jump out. Smooth on our Body Yogurt. Jump in your jeans. Get on with your summer.* As it can be seen, each sentence is started with a verb in the same grammatical form.

b. Advertisement made by ChatGPT 3.5
Prompt: *Please write a short description for the website advertisement for the Refreshing Passionfruit Body Yogurt by Body Shop. Please select and use some linguistic measures from semantic/syntactic/rhetorical level. Below the description, please indicate what types of linguistic measures you used and what is their objective in this advertisement.*

**BOX 5.17   THE BODY SHOP, BODY YOGHURT –
ADVERTISEMENT BY CHATGPT 3.5**

Indulge in Refreshing Passionfruit Bliss with The Body Shop Body Yogurt

Escape to a tropical paradise with The Body Shop's Refreshing Passionfruit Body Yogurt. Infused with the essence of sun-kissed passionfruit, this lightweight, gel-cream formula absorbs instantly, leaving your skin feeling hydrated, smooth, and delicately scented. Perfect for hot summer days or whenever your skin needs a burst of fruity freshness.

Linguistic measures used:

1. Evocative adjectives: "Refreshing", "sun-kissed", "delicately scented" – These adjectives are chosen to evoke sensory experiences and positive associations with the product, emphasising its refreshing and pleasant qualities.
2. Vivid imagery: "Escape to a tropical paradise", "burst of fruity freshness" – These phrases create vivid imagery and appeal to consumers' desires for a rejuvenating and uplifting skincare experience.
3. Consumer benefit: "Absorbs instantly", "hydrated, smooth skin" – These statements highlight practical benefits, addressing consumer concerns such as hydration and texture without feeling heavy or greasy.

Objectives in advertisement:

- Creating desire: The use of evocative adjectives and vivid imagery aims to create desire and appeal to consumers' aspirations for a refreshing and pleasant skincare experience.
- Highlighting benefits: By emphasising the quick absorption and hydrating properties, the advertisement aims to persuade consumers of the practical benefits of using the Body Yogurt, positioning it as an effective and convenient skincare choice.
- Setting a scene: Phrases like "escape to a tropical paradise" set a scene and transport consumers to a desirable state of mind, enhancing the emotional connection with the product.

The above-mentioned commercial produced by ChatGPT in version 3.5 is not particularly linguistically extensive, but AI has succeeded in developing thought-provoking sentences and words that evoke vivid images in the consumer's mind.

The objectives are well-composed and fairly distributed, with a total of five. ChatGPT's objectives include *creating desire*, *highlighting benefits*, and *setting a scene*. What is remarkable, however, is that the list of "linguistic measures used" also included objectives rather than linguistic measures. These are *vivid imagery* and *consumer benefit*. All of the above explains that the advertisement for this product is intended to stimulate vivid imagination, arouse desire, highlight practical benefits, and enhance the emotional connection with the product.

The point was mentioned that this advertisement does not have many linguistic measures. It only has them at the lexical level. Of those mentioned by ChatGPT, these are evocative (favourable) adjectives such as *refreshing*, *sun-kissed*, and *delicately scented*. Also worth adding to this list are *hydrated*, *lightweight,* and *smooth*. In addition, not already mentioned, there are as many as three compounds, i.e. *gel-cream*, and the previously mentioned *sun-kissed* and *lightweight*. This number of compounds adds dynamism to the entire advertisement. ChatGPT also managed to include one personal pronoun *your*, which makes the advertisement a direct message to the consumer.

As stated earlier, the above-mentioned advertisement does not have many linguistic measures. As a result, it is not a strongly persuasive advertisement either, as its linguistic measures are only on one level – lexical.

c. Advertisement made by ChatGPT 4.0

**BOX 5.18 THE BODY SHOP, BODY YOGHURT –
ADVERTISEMENT BY CHATGPT 4.0**

Dive into a tropical treat with The Body Shop's Refreshing Passionfruit Body Yogurt. This fast-absorbing, lightweight formula revitalizes your skin with a burst of zesty passionfruit essence. Perfect for a quick, hydrating escape, our body yogurt leaves your skin silky, not sticky. Enjoy instant moisture and a delightful scent that lingers, transforming your daily skincare into an exotic indulgence.

Linguistic measures used:

1. Metaphor (rhetorical level): Describing the body yogurt as a "tropical treat" uses a metaphor that transports consumers to an exotic locale through sensory experience. This metaphor enhances the appeal by associating the product with relaxation and pleasure.
2. Imperative sentence (syntactic level): "Dive into" serves as an imperative, inviting the consumer to immerse themselves in the experience of using the product. This direct command engages the reader and encourages immediate action or interest.
3. Positive adjectives (lexical level): Words like "refreshing", "lightweight", "silky", and "delightful" positively frame the product, highlighting its desirable qualities and benefits. These adjectives create an attractive image of the product and enhance consumer appeal.
4. Alliteration (rhetorical level): The phrase "fast-absorbing, lightweight formula" uses alliteration to make the description more rhythmic and memorable, which can enhance retention and enjoyment of the text.
5. Personification (rhetorical level): By stating the scent "lingers", there is a subtle use of personification, giving a human-like quality to the fragrance. This suggests that the scent has a presence and character, enhancing the sensory appeal of the product.

ChatGPT 4.0 performed well with the Body Yoghurt product advertisement by The Body Shop brand. The linguistic measures, in contrast to the previous advertisement, appeared on all three levels, which strongly may lead to an increase in consumer purchase willingness.

Linguistic measures used and correctly identified were the metaphor, imperative sentence, and positive adjectives. Furthermore, it is observable that there are slightly more linguistic measures than those listed. These include personal pronouns, again in a *your-our* relationship, designed to build a bond and make the advertisement easier to digest. Compounds such as *fast-absorbing* and *lightweight* were also used, as well as the single weasel word *revitalises*, which suggests that the product may invigorate our skin, although it does not have to be this way at all and that might signal a slight manipulation already.

In terms of mistakes, there were only a few. The most shocking one was the alleged alliteration in the phrase *fast-absorbing, lightweight formula*, which under no circumstances repeats letters after each other and is therefore not an alliteration. Another was the misidentification of personification, since the verb *lingers* also functions about the fragrance meaning "to continue to exist for a long time and often much longer than expected".[4] One further point worth mentioning is *hydrating escape*. The phrase just sounds unnatural and bizarre, and the two words do not quite go hand in hand.

Example 2

a. Advertisement made by a human

> ### BOX 5.19   THE BODY SHOP, SHOWER GEL – ADVERTISEMENT BY A HUMAN
>
> *Lather up with our special edition Cool Daisy Shower Gel to leave you and your skin feeling nicely cleansed and smelling as fresh as a daisy. It's one of our freshest, brightest and, well, coolest scents ever. It's like wandering through a field of daisies, or a festival (but one of the chilled-out, daytime ones).*

As it can be seen, The Body Shop it is not persuasive on a syntactic level as it has long and complex sentences. However, regarding lexical and rhetorical levels, it can be persuasive and manipulative.

Taking into consideration the lexical level there is a weasel word, personal pronouns, and a favourable superlative degree. As for the weasel word the advertiser makes use of the verb <u>*to leave*</u> you, which has the meaning of the promise to give our skin "feeling nicely cleansed and smelling as fresh as a daisy". In fact, the advertiser cannot guarantee that but implies that the product will actually help. The commercial also shortens the distance between the advertiser and the consumer by employing personal pronouns such as *our, you, your*. In addition, it has recourse to favourable superlative degree in adjectives – *freshest, brightest*, and *coolest*. These adjectives introduce competitive technique. Advertisers highlight features that make their items appear superior to similar products from competitors.

Furthermore, in The Body Shop advertisement, two similes occur regarding the rhetorical level. The first one is *smelling as fresh as daisy* and the second one is *it's like wandering through field of daisies*. Since the scent of the product is like the scent of flowers, these two similes relate to our senses. By making these comparisons, the advertiser persuades us to make a purchase even more because it appeals to our imagination.

b. Advertisement made by ChatGPT 3.5
Prompt: *Please write a short description for the website advertisement for the Cool Daisy Shower Gel from the Body Shop. Please select and use some linguistic measures from semantic/syntactic/rhetorical level. Below the description, please indicate what types of linguistic measures you used and what is their objective in this advertisement.*

BOX 5.20   THE BODY SHOP, SHOWER GEL – ADVERTISEMENT CHATGPT 3.5

Embrace Freshness with Cool Daisy Shower Gel from The Body Shop
Indulge your senses in the refreshing essence of Cool Daisy Shower Gel by The Body Shop. Enriched with daisy extract, this invigorating formula gently cleanses and revitalizes your skin, leaving it feeling fresh and delicately scented. Immerse yourself in a shower experience that uplifts your mood and rejuvenates your senses. Elevate your daily routine with the floral freshness of Cool Daisy Shower Gel and let your skin glow with renewed vitality.

Linguistic measures used:

1. Evocative adjectives: "Refreshing", "invigorating", "fresh", "delicately scented", "uplifts", "rejuvenates", "glow with renewed vitality" – These adjectives evoke a sensory experience and highlight the product's benefits, emphasising freshness, rejuvenation, and fragrance.
2. Imperatives: "Embrace", "Indulge", "Immerse", "Elevate" – Imperatives encourage action and engagement, urging the reader to experience the product and its benefits first-hand.

3. Sensory language: "Refreshing essence", "uplifts your mood", "rejuvenates your senses", "delicately scented" – Descriptive language that appeals to the senses creates a vivid image of the product experience, enhancing its appeal.

Objectives in advertisement:

- Creating sensory appeal: The use of evocative adjectives and sensory language aims to create an emotional connection with the reader, enticing them to imagine and desire the refreshing experience of using Cool Daisy Shower Gel.
- Encouraging engagement: Imperatives like "Embrace" and "Indulge" encourage immediate engagement with the product, urging consumers to consider incorporating it into their daily routine.
- Highlighting benefits: By emphasising the product's ability to cleanse, revitalise, and leave skin delicately scented, the advertisement aims to highlight the practical benefits of using Cool Daisy Shower Gel.

In this particular advertisement, ChatGPT 3.5 hauntingly managed to identify the linguistic measures used. All those listed were present in the advertisement. What was missing, however, was the mention of the personal pronoun *your,* which appeared four times, and the weasel words, i.e. *revitalises, uplifts*, and *rejuvenates*, which suggest that the product can fulfil certain qualities, although this is not necessarily true as it cannot be clearly identified.

Additionally, the advertisement generated by the AI posed the objectives superbly and accurately. It is rather impossible to dispute any of them. The objectives posed result in a highly persuasive advertisement. Unfortunately, no measures appeared at the rhetorical level and only one at the syntactic level, and long and elaborate sentences can be hard to comprehend for some consumers. Fortunately, they are mostly imperative, so the persuasive function will continue to be fulfilled.

All in all, this is an admirably composed advertisement. Despite the lack of rhetorical measures, it continues to be strongly convincing, and due to the weasel words, it can also be considered manipulative.

c. Advertisement made by ChatGPT 4.0

> **BOX 5.21   THE BODY SHOP, SHOWER GEL –**
> **ADVERTISEMENT BY CHATGPT 4.0**
>
> *Awaken your senses with The Body Shop's Cool Daisy Shower Gel. Infused with the crisp, refreshing scent of daisies, this shower gel offers a cleansing experience that revitalizes both body and mind. Its invigorating formula washes away the stresses of the day, leaving your skin feeling fresh and renewed. Step into your shower and let the cool daisy embrace envelop you in its soothing freshness – every day is a new bloom.*
>
> Linguistic measures used:
>
> 1. Personification (rhetorical level): The phrase "let the cool daisy embrace envelop you" personifies the scent of the shower gel, suggesting it has the ability to wrap around and comfort the user. This approach adds a nurturing, almost protective quality to the product, enhancing its appeal.
> 2. Metaphor (rhetorical level): Referring to "every day is a new bloom" employs a metaphor that links daily showering with the freshness and renewal of a blooming flower. This metaphor enhances the product's value by associating it with growth and new beginnings, which is emotionally uplifting.
> 3. Positive adjectives (lexical level): Using adjectives like "crisp", "refreshing", "invigorating", and "soothing" creates a vivid and attractive description that highlights the sensory benefits of the product, making it more appealing to potential buyers.
> 4. Imperative sentence (syntactic level): "Step into your shower" is an imperative sentence that not only instructs but also invites the reader to use the product, creating a call to action that is engaging and direct.
> 5. Alliteration (rhetorical level): The repetition of the "s" sound in "soothing freshness" makes the description smooth and pleasing to the ear, which can make the overall reading experience more enjoyable and the text more memorable.

As for the first impression of the advertisement proposed by version 4.0, it is a very well-written advertisement that influences the consumer's senses. Moreover, four of the five measures are correctly identified and assigned to the appropriate levels. However, these are not all that appeared in the advertisement.

In the context of the linguistic measures presented in the list of "linguistic measures used":

1. The personification was correctly presented, as was its objective. The only puzzling thing is the juxtaposition of two verbs (*embrace* and *envelop*) next to each other as it is not grammatically correct and they mean the same thing.
2. The metaphor *everyday is a new bloom* is excellent. Beautifully composed and very persuasive.
3. Advertisement has lots of positive (favourable) verbs. Yet the ones listed by ChatGPT are only four out of seven. The other three are *cleansing, fresh*, and *renewed*.
4. The sentence *Step into your shower* is indeed imperative, but not the only one functioning as such. The advertisement also features a second imperative sentence *Awaken your senses*, which introduces us to a daisy-scented world.
5. As it turns out again, ChatGPT has serious issues with identifying alliteration – it identifies it when indeed there is none. Thus, the phrase *soothing freshness* is not an alliteration.

In addition to the above, it can be added that the personal nouns *your* and *you* also appeared in the advertisement. Unfortunately, the advertisement lacks simple sentences, so it turns overcomplicated. However, this does not significantly affect its overall reception, as the first and last sentences wonderfully open and close advertisement. More importantly, the last sentence features the monosyllabic verbs *step* and *let* along with the previously discussed metaphor – creating a highly memorable message.

Example 3

a. Advertisement made by a human

BOX 5.22   GARNIER, HAIR MASK – ADVERTISEMENT BY A HUMAN

Hangry, Fine Hair? Dig into our Garnier Ultimate Blends Plumping Hair Food Watermelon Hair Mask Treatment to leave hair looking boosted and feeling plumped. It's intensely hydrating formula and melting texture instantly absorbs into hair with no weigh down.

The opening sentence in this advertisement grabs considerable attention. On a syntactical level, it is short, minor, and interrogative at the same time. It is very easy to read (as it consists of only three words), catchy, and visually appealing. When it comes to the rhetorical level, this sentence also contains a personification – *hangry hair*. Hangry is a blend of words hungry and angry and in informal language means "irritable or angry because of hunger".[5] Due to this personification, the advertiser creates greater interest in the product since consumers will seek to use something that could "feed" their hair.

However, these are not the only elements of trickery in this advertisement. It also appeared on the lexical level. The personal pronoun *our* appears, which makes the advertisement more direct and the consumer is more likely to respond. Then, by employing the same weasel word as it was in the example number 4 – *to leave hair looking boosted and feeling plumped*, the advertiser makes a promise that will not necessarily be fulfilled. Last but not least, this commercial makes use of contrasting adjectives. The negative adjectives (*hangry, fine*) are answered by the positive ones (*boosted, plumped*). *Hangry* and *fine* hair are connected to difficulties that existed before buying the product and *boosted* and *plumped* hair can be the result of using it.

b. Advertisement made by ChatGPT 3.5
Prompt: *Please write a short description for the website advertisement for the Garnier Ultimate Blends Plumping Hair Food Watermelon Hair Mask. Please select and use some linguistic measures from semantic/syntactic/rhetorical level. Below the description, please indicate what types of linguistic measures you used and what is their objective in this advertisement.*

BOX 5.23   GARNIER, HAIR MASK – ADVERTISEMENT BY CHATGPT 3.5

Indulge Your Hair with Garnier Ultimate Blends Plumping Hair Food Watermelon Hair Mask
    Revitalize your hair with the refreshing Garnier Ultimate Blends Plumping Hair Food Watermelon Hair Mask. Enriched with watermelon extract and plant proteins, this nourishing mask deeply hydrates and adds volume to fine, flat hair. Experience hair that feels visibly plumped and full of life, with a deliciously fruity fragrance that lingers. Treat your locks to a burst of hydration and bounce, leaving them irresistibly soft and beautifully fragrant after each use.

Linguistic measures used:

Semantic level:

- Positive adjectives: "Refreshing", "nourishing", "hydrates", "adds volume", "plumped", "full of life", "irresistibly soft", "beautifully fragrant". These adjectives evoke positive sensory experiences and benefits associated with using the hair mask.
- Specific ingredients: "Watermelon extract", "plant proteins". Highlighting key ingredients known for their hydrating and volumising properties appeals to consumers seeking natural-based hair care solutions.

Syntactic level:

- Parallel structure: "Treat your locks to a burst of hydration and bounce, leaving them irresistibly soft and beautifully fragrant after each use." This structure emphasises the dual benefits of hydration and fragrance, reinforcing the mask's effectiveness.
- Descriptive phrases: "Enriched with watermelon extract and plant proteins", "deliciously fruity fragrance". These phrases provide detailed information about the mask's formulation and sensory appeal.

Rhetorical level:

- Imagery: "Indulge Your Hair", "burst of hydration and bounce", "visibly plumped and full of life". These phrases create vivid mental images and sensory experiences, enhancing the appeal of the hair mask.
- Alliteration: "Plumping Hair Food Watermelon Hair Mask" adds a rhythmic quality and emphasises the main ingredients and benefits.
- Direct address: "Treat your locks" directly engages the consumer, inviting them to experience the benefits of the hair mask firsthand.

Objectives:

Semantic level: The use of positive adjectives and specific ingredients aims to highlight the mask's benefits, such as hydration, volume, and fragrance, appealing to consumers looking to improve the condition and appearance of their hair.

Syntactic level: Parallel structure and descriptive phrases enhance clarity and effectiveness in communicating the mask's benefits and formulation, promoting its appeal and usability.

Rhetorical level: Imagery, alliteration, and direct address enhance the mask's appeal and memorability, encouraging consumer engagement and purchase by emphasising its natural ingredients and beneficial effects on hair health.

In this advertisement, ChatGPT 3.5 correctly distinguished and identified only three linguistic measures, as the rest of the listed measures were not linguistic measures. Those correctly identified were descriptive phrases, imagery, and positive adjectives. In the latter, unfortunately, a minor mistake crept in, as the list compiled by Chat included the phrase *adds volume*, which is in absolutely no way an adjective.

Measures not identified by ChatGPT but present in the advertisement are as follows:

1. *Feels*, *adds*, and *treat* – As monosyllabic verbs that support the readability and comprehensibility of the advertisement.
2. *Full of life* – A personification that refers to hair and in its context means hair that is thick and full of shine
3. *Fine, flat hair* – This is both an alliteration and a negative adjective. As well as adding rhythm, it simultaneously creates the suggestion that, as a result of using the advertised product, the hair will cease to have these qualities.

Overall, the advertisement is correct and its objectives are also not questionable in terms of correctness as well as agreeing with the content of the advertisement. However, it is not a very linguistically extensive advertisement, hence, despite everything, its message will not be as persuasive as it could be.

c. Advertisement made by ChatGPT 4.0

BOX 5.24 GARNIER, HAIR MASK – ADVERTISEMENT BY CHATGPT 4.0

Quench your hair's thirst with Garnier Ultimate Blends Plumping Hair Food Watermelon Hair Mask. Bursting with the juicy freshness of watermelon, this hair mask deeply hydrates and plumps each strand, delivering luscious, voluminous results. It's the perfect recipe for hair that looks as healthy and vibrant as it feels. Dive into the succulence of watermelon and watch your hair transform into a lush, bouncy mane.

Linguistic measures used:

1. Metaphor (rhetorical level): Describing the mask as "Quench your hair's thirst" uses a metaphor that personifies hair as having needs similar to a living creature, emphasising the nourishing and satisfying effect of the product. This connection enhances the perceived efficacy of the hair mask.
2. Alliteration (rhetorical level): The phrase "perfect recipe for hair" employs alliteration with the repetition of the "p" sound, making the text more engaging and memorable for the reader.
3. Imperative sentence (syntactic level): "Dive into the succulence of watermelon" is an imperative sentence that encourages action, inviting the consumer to experience the product firsthand. This call to action is designed to motivate immediate interest and use.
4. Positive adjectives (lexical level): Adjectives like "juicy", "luscious", "vibrant", and "bouncy" create a vivid and attractive image of the product's benefits, appealing directly to the consumer's desire for appealing sensory experiences and effective results.
5. Personification (rhetorical level): The phrase "watch your hair transform into a lush, bouncy mane" personifies hair by suggesting it can undergo a dramatic, almost magical transformation. This enhances the allure of the product by promising significant and desirable changes.

The advertisement appears to be an excellent option for summer. Its persuasive nature strongly encourages consumers to purchase the product immediately upon reading. On the more technical aspect, ChatGPT has mostly managed to identify the measures it used, although there were a couple of mistakes.

From a rhetorical perspective, it is important to correct that the metaphor identified by ChatGPT is actually a personification. The true metaphor in the advertisement is *dive into the succulence of watermelon*, which vividly enhances the text by evoking summertime imagery and suggesting the hydration benefits of the product. Additionally, the personification *watch your hair transform into a lush, bouncy mane*, correctly identified by ChatGPT, is effectively persuasive and accurately employs this rhetorical device.

The positive adjectives are also noteworthy, encompassing more than just *juicy, luscious, vibrant,* and *bouncy.* Terms such as *plumping, voluminous, perfect,* and *healthy* also fall into this category. On the lexical level, monosyllabic verbs not initially highlighted by ChatGPT but frequently employed include *quench, plumps, looks, feels,* and *watch.* The use of five such verbs is quite notable for an AI-generated advertisement.

At the syntactic level, there are two imperative sentences. The first, identified by the AI, is *Dive into the succulence of watermelon,* while the second, previously unmentioned, is *Quench your hair's thirst.* Both sentences are persuasive, encouraging the consumer to take action leading to the purchase of the product.

The only notable drawback of this advertisement is the complexity of its sentences. However, the effectiveness of the other linguistic devices compensates for this, resulting in an overall highly effective advertisement.

Example 4

a. Advertisement made by a human

**BOX 5.25   JANSSEN COSMETICS, SERUM –
ADVERTISEMENT BY A HUMAN**

Skin-smoothing active ingredient serum for mature skin with the Cellular Regeneration Complex of red clover extract and Kombucha. The high-performance complex ensures an extensive regeneration of the skin, smooths it and improves its radiance. The highly-concentrated formula for during the day is the ideal complement to the Mature Skin care creams.

The above-mentioned example is not persuasive on a syntactic level but can be concerning lexical and rhetorical aspects. Starting from rhetorical aspects, it contains the euphemism – *mature skin.* The advertiser replaces the biological decay (*old*) with maturity. As it was said in Chapter 2, in the language of advertising, euphemism is used to mitigate uncomfortable issues to present a more positive image. In this case, an uncomfortable issue is *old skin* and a more positive image is *mature skin.*

The possible effects of persuasion are visible on the lexical level. First of all, there are favourable adjectives divided into two groups: compounds and coinage neologisms. *Skin-smoothing* adjective is the compound that gives the advertising message more dynamism and elicits rich associations in recipients. *High-performance* and *highly-concentrated* are adjectives that can be categorised as coinage neologisms. They may imply that the product has unusual qualities and is innovative. Weasel word – *ensures* – is also used as a manipulative tool. By *ensuring an extensive regeneration of the skin*, the advertiser avoids making a direct statement that makes their declaration only a suggestion, but in which consumers will believe and want to have the product anyway.

b. Advertisement made by ChatGPT 3.5
Prompt: *Please write a short description for the website advertisement for the Cellular Regeneration Complex by Janssen Cosmetics. Please select and use some linguistic measures from semantic/syntactic/rhetorical level. Below the description, please indicate what types of linguistic measures you used and what is their objective in this advertisement.*

**BOX 5.26   JANSSEN COSMETICS, SERUM –
ADVERTISEMENT BY CHATGPT 3.5**

Rediscover Youthful Radiance with Janssen Cosmetics Cellular Regeneration Complex
  Indulge in the pinnacle of skincare innovation with Janssen Cosmetics' Cellular Regeneration Complex. This state-of-the-art formula harnesses groundbreaking technology to deeply nourish and regenerate your skin at a cellular level. Enriched with potent antioxidants and revitalizing peptides, it counteracts signs of aging, enhances skin elasticity, and promotes a luminous, youthful complexion.

Linguistic measures used:

1. Technical terminology: "Cellular Regeneration Complex" and "groundbreaking technology" utilise technical language to convey advanced scientific development and efficacy, appealing to consumers interested in cutting-edge skincare solutions.
2. Descriptive adjectives: "Potent", "revitalizing", "luminous", "youthful complexion" – These adjectives evoke strong positive associations, emphasising the powerful effects of the product and promising visible improvements in skin appearance.
3. Scientific claims: "Deeply nourish", "regenerate at a cellular level", "counteract signs of aging", "enhance skin elasticity" – These claims are rooted in scientific benefits, appealing to consumers seeking evidence-based skincare solutions.

Objectives in advertisement:

- Establishing authority: By using technical terminology and scientific claims, the advertisement establishes the product's authority and credibility in the skincare market, appealing to discerning consumers who value scientific innovation.
- Highlighting benefits: The emphasis on descriptive adjectives and scientific claims highlights the transformative benefits of the Cellular Regeneration Complex, compelling consumers to consider it for achieving radiant, youthful-looking skin.
- Targeting concerns: Addressing concerns such as ageing signs and skin elasticity, the advertisement targets consumers looking for effective solutions to specific skincare challenges, positioning the product as an essential component of a comprehensive skincare routine.

The advertisement for the serum from Janssen Cosmetics is linguistically sophisticated and well-composed. However, ChatGPT version 3.5 was unable to identify the linguistic measures it employed, except for descriptive adjectives. The objectives, however, were well articulated.

The advertisement utilised several linguistic measures, including the following:

1. The weasel word *rediscover* in the phrase *rediscover youthful radiance*. The choice of *rediscover* instead of *discover* might imply that the product is targeted primarily at older individuals. However, considering that everyone's skin has different needs, younger individuals might also be inclined to use this product.
2. The compound *state-of-the-art*, which evokes rich associations in consumers.
3. Hyperbole in the phrase *groundbreaking technology,* which emphasises the supposed innovation and revolutionary nature of the product. This creates even stronger associations in consumers than the previous compound.
4. The euphemism *signs of aging*, which softens the unpleasant connotations associated with becoming or being "old". While the word "old" often carries negative associations, *signs of aging* is phrased more gently and carries a different, more positive nuance.
5. An imperative sentence that is also simple and concise: *Rediscover youthful radiance with Janssen Cosmetics Cellular Regeneration*

Complex. This sentence's multifunctionality at the syntactic level, combined with its prominent placement at the beginning of the advertisement, makes it highly persuasive.

Overall, despite the lack of accurate identification of linguistic devices, this advertisement is well-crafted and complex as for ChatGPT 3.5.

c. Advertisement made by ChatGPT 4.0

**BOX 5.27   JANSSEN COSMETICS, SERUM –
ADVERTISEMENT BY CHATGPT 4.0**

Revitalize your skin's essence with Janssen Cosmetics' Cellular Regeneration Complex. This revolutionary serum harnesses the power of advanced science to rejuvenate your cells and unveil a youthful glow. Experience the magic of deep cellular renewal as this potent formula targets signs of aging and restores vitality. With each application, reveal a smoother, firmer, and more radiant complexion. Trust in the science of beauty to turn back time.

Linguistic measures used:

1. Metaphor (rhetorical level): The phrases "Revitalize your skin's essence" and "the magic of deep cellular renewal" employ metaphors that elevate the product's effects to a more mystical, almost magical level, enhancing the perceived potency and allure of the serum.
2. Alliteration (rhetorical level): "Smoother, firmer, and more radiant" uses alliteration with the repetition of the "r" sound, creating a pleasing rhythm and enhancing the text's memorability.
3. Imperative sentence (syntactic level): "Trust in the science of beauty" is an imperative sentence that not only instructs but also builds confidence in the product's scientific foundation, encouraging users to rely on the product for anti-ageing solutions.
4. Positive adjectives (lexical level): Words like "revolutionary", "youthful", "potent", and "radiant" positively frame the product, highlighting its innovative and effective qualities. These adjectives build a strong appeal by emphasising the transformative effects of the serum.
5. Hyperbole (rhetorical level): "Turn back time" is a hyperbolic statement that exaggerates the product's benefits to create a strong

emotional impact. This hyperbole aims to convey the effectiveness of the serum in fighting signs of ageing, making it highly desirable for its rejuvenating properties.

The above-mentioned advertisement is well-composed, where ChatGPT 4.0 correctly identified 80% of the linguistic measures shown on the list it made. The remaining 20%, which ChatGPT did not correctly identify, included alliteration. ChatGPT mistakenly identified the "r" sound in the phrase *smoother, firmer, and more radiant* as alliteration, which it is not, since it does not repeat an initial syllable.

The identified linguistic measures – metaphor, imperative sentence, positive adjectives, and hyperbole – are part of the accurately identified 80%. They have been correctly matched to their respective levels. Notably, the hyperbole *turn back time* should be highlighted, with its objective clearly presented. This phrase is likely to be memorable and is therefore highly persuasive.

However, the advertisement also included linguistic measures not distinguished by ChatGPT:

1. Weasel word *rejuvenate your cells*, which suggests that the product will help improve the visual signs of ageing at a cellular level.
2. Euphemism *signs of aging*, which emphasises the goal of maintaining or restoring a more youthful look and simultaneously avoids the direct mention of being old.
3. Comparative degree *smoother, firmer, and more radiant complexion*, which can effectively set the product apart from competitors by showcasing its superior benefits.

As may be noted, the advertisement proposed by version 4.0 has a lot of linguistic measures, yet many of them were identified by ChatGPT itself.

Example 5

a. Advertisement made by a human

BOX 5.28   AESOP, EYE SERUM – ADVERTISEMENT BY A HUMAN

A feast for the eyes. Infused with vitamins and readily absorbed, this high-potency formulation delivers sustained hydration to the skin around the eyes – a delicate, dryness-prone, and easily depleted area.

The above-mentioned advertisement is short but carries persuasive tools. Referring to the first sentence, on the syntactic level it is a minor sentence and its aim is to emphasise the quality of the product. On the rhetorical one, it is a metaphor. *A feast for the eyes* can be taken literally but also figuratively. In the literal sense, the eye serum will bring a lot of nutrients to our skin. On the other hand, in the figurative sense, it means "an especially attractive, pleasing, or remarkable sight or visual experience",[6] what may refer to the product packaging or its contents. As it can be seen, the advertiser employs a word game that the customer will undoubtedly remember, increasing the likelihood of purchasing the product.

Although this advertisement's persuasiveness is mostly built on the metaphor, it also manifests itself on a lexical level. The weasel word (*delivers sustained hydration*) manipulates and appears again to make the consumer believe in something that is probably not true. Innovation of the products is shown by the compound *dryness-prone* and the coinage neologism *high-potency*.

b. Advertisement made by ChatGPT 3.5
Prompt: *Please write a short description for the eye serum by Aesop for the website advertisement. Please select and use some linguistic measures from semantic/syntactic/rhetorical level. Below the description, please indicate what types of linguistic measures you used and what is their objective in this advertisement.*

BOX 5.29   AESOP, EYE SERUM – ADVERTISEMENT BY CHATGPT 3.5

Rejuvenate Your Eyes with Aesop Parsley Seed Anti-Oxidant Eye Serum
   Nourish and protect the delicate skin around your eyes with Aesop's Parsley Seed Anti-Oxidant Eye Serum. Enriched with botanical extracts rich in antioxidants, this rejuvenating serum delivers essential hydration and revitalizes tired eyes. Perfect for all skin types, it gently cares for your skin, leaving it refreshed and radiant.

Linguistic measures used:

Semantic level:

- Positive adjectives: "Rejuvenate", "nourish", "protect", "rich in antioxidants", "essential hydration", "revitalizes", "refreshed", "radiant".

- Domain-specific terms: "Botanical extracts", "antioxidants", "delicate skin", "rejuvenating serum". These terms establish expertise and credibility in skincare.
- Ethical appeal: Emphasising natural ingredients and suitability for all skin types aligns with ethical consumer preferences.

Syntactic level:

- Compound sentences: "Enriched with botanical extracts rich in antioxidants, this rejuvenating serum delivers essential hydration and revitalizes tired eyes." This structure connects related ideas to highlight benefits clearly.
- Parallel structure: "Rejuvenate Your Eyes", "Nourish and protect", "Perfect for all skin types". This creates a rhythmic flow and emphasises key selling points.

Rhetorical level:

- Metaphor: "Rejuvenate Your Eyes" compares using the serum to a process of revitalisation, enhancing its appeal.
- Repetition: "Rejuvenate", "nourish", "protect", "revitalizes", "refreshed", "radiant". This repetition reinforces the positive effects of the serum, making the advertisement more persuasive.
- Direct address: "Perfect for all skin types." This directly addresses potential concerns about compatibility, reassuring the audience.

Objectives:

Semantic level: The positive adjectives and domain-specific terms aim to convey the serum's effectiveness, natural ingredients, and suitability for diverse skin types.

Syntactic level: Compound sentences and parallel structure enhance readability and emphasise key benefits, ensuring the advertisement is informative and engaging.

Rhetorical level: Metaphor and repetition enhance the serum's appeal and memorability, while direct address reassures potential customers of its broad applicability.

The advertisement generated by ChatGPT 3.5 is brief and to the point. However, despite its conciseness, it incorporates numerous persuasive linguistic strategies. Unfortunately, these strategies are largely misidentified by the AI, necessitating independent identification by the user.

At the semantic level, the AI accurately identifies domain-specific terms, which enhance the advertisement's credibility. Nevertheless, it incorrectly categorises "ethical appeal", which should not be considered a linguistic measure but rather an objective. Furthermore, while the AI notes the presence of positive adjectives, listing six such adjectives (i.e. *delicate, botanical, rejuvenating, essential, refreshed, radiant*), it predominantly misclassifies verbs (e.g., *nourish, protect, rejuvenate*) as adjectives.

At the syntactic level, ChatGPT has adequately identified compound sentences. However, it is well-documented that longer sentences can be more challenging for consumers to process, which diminishes the advertisement's persuasiveness. The goal at this level is also misrepresented, as compound sentences do not necessarily improve readability.

At the rhetorical level, there are two incorrect identifications and one correct one. The first misidentification is repetition, defined as the multiple occurrences of a word or phrase, which is absent in the provided example. The second misidentification is direct address, which is not present in the advertisement. Only the identification of metaphor is correct.

However, as previously mentioned, this advertisement contains several additional linguistic measures. These include the following:

1. The weasel word in the phrase *rejuvenate your eyes*, where *rejuvenate* suggests revitalisation and refreshment of the eyes, although the product may not have the same effect on everyone. This is a manipulative linguistic measure.
2. Alliteration in *refreshed and radiant*, where the repetition of the "r" sound adds rhythm and memorability.
3. The negative adjective in the phrase *tired eyes*, highlighting the problem that the product aims to solve. Negative adjectives intensify the impact of positive adjectives through contrast.
4. Coinage neologism and compound *anti-oxidant*, which makes the advertisement more interesting and eye-catching.

In conclusion, despite some identification errors, this advertisement remains linguistically rich. Given its brevity and the number of linguistic measures it incorporates, it can be considered highly persuasive.

c. Advertisement made by ChatGPT 4.0

BOX 5.30   AESOP, EYE SERUM – ADVERTISEMENT BY CHATGPT 4.0

Illuminate your gaze with Aesop's advanced eye serum. This meticulously crafted formula targets the delicate skin around your eyes, smoothing fine lines and reducing puffiness with its rich, botanical essences. Every drop delivers a profound transformation, awakening your eyes to a refreshed and youthful appearance. Embrace the art of subtlety and reveal your brightest, most serene eyes.

Linguistic measures used:

1. Alliteration (rhetorical level): The phrase "profound transformation" uses alliteration with the repetition of the "p" sound, enhancing the auditory quality of the description and making it more memorable and impactful.
2. Metaphor (rhetorical level): Describing the serum as having the "art of subtlety" employs a metaphor that elevates the product to a fine art form, implying it is both sophisticated and effective in gently enhancing the skin's appearance.
3. Imperative sentence (syntactic level): "Embrace the art of subtlety" is an imperative sentence that invites the consumer to experience the serum's gentle and effective treatment. This command engages the reader directly, encouraging them to take action.
4. Positive adjectives (lexical level): Words like "advanced", "rich", "refreshed", and "youthful" positively frame the serum, emphasising its effectiveness and appealing directly to the consumer's desire for high-quality skincare products.
5. Personification (rhetorical level): "Awakening your eyes" personifies the eyes, suggesting that they can be "awoken" or revitalised by the serum. This personification creates a vivid image of the benefits, enhancing the product's appeal by attributing human characteristics to the results.

The advertisement generated by ChatGPT version 4.0 is another relatively short piece. Despite its brevity, similar to the version 3.5 advertisement, it is linguistically rich. In this instance, the AI performed better in identifying the linguistic measures employed.

The only error made by the AI is the incorrect identification of alliteration. ChatGPT suggested that the phrase *profound transformation* is an alliteration; however, no letters or sounds are repeated in succession.

On a rhetorical level, the AI successfully identified and created metaphors and personification. These linguistic measures generate vivid images and enhance the product's appeal. Additionally, there is another metaphor – *every drop delivers a profound transformation* – which could also serve as a compelling slogan.

The AI correctly identified imperative sentences, such as *Embrace the art of subtlety*, and there is another imperative sentence, *Illuminate your gaze*. These two sentences work brilliantly together, serving as the opening and closing statements of the advertisement.

ChatGPT 4.0 also utilised and identified positive adjectives, namely *advanced, rich, refreshed*, and *youthful*. However, there are an additional five adjectives present: *delicate, botanical, profound, brightest*, and *serene*. Additionally, the phrase *your brightest, most serene eyes* serves as a superlative degree and through the use of the personal pronoun *your* directly addresses the consumer, enhancing its persuasiveness.

Example 6

a. Advertisement made by a human

BOX 5.31   FACE REALITY, TONER – ADVERTISEMENT BY A HUMAN

Have some serious acne breakouts? Well, here's a serious toner. It is exfoliating, anti-inflammatory, brightening, and provides antioxidant support for the skin. This multi-functional toner contains L-Ascorbic acid, which is a highly effective, stabilized version of vitamin C. It is recommended for skin prone to all types of acne and acne rosacea, but especially inflamed acne. The anti-inflammatory and exfoliating quality of this toner will seriously help get it under control.

Despite that this advertisement does not have any linguistic features on a rhetorical level, it does on the lexical and syntactical one. In the matter of syntactic level, the first two sentences achieve persuasive and memorable effect. *Have some serious acne breakouts?* – this sentence is interrogative, simple, short, and minor at the same time. The next one (*Well, here's a serious toner*) can be classified as simple and short. The first sentence brings up a question that will probably be answered in the affirmative if the consumer is looking for an acne treatment product, and the second sentence brings up a solution to this problem. In the second sentence, it can also be understood that the advertiser gave themselves the answer to the question in the first sentence.

Referring to the lexical level, some monosyllabic verbs were introduced such as *have, help,* and *get.* The weasel word – *help* – emerges again here, as it did in the prior examples. It also includes adjectives such as *exfoliating, anti-inflammatory, brightening, multi-functional,* and *effective.* What is more, the advertisement contains coinage neologisms – *antioxidant, anti-inflammatory,* and *multi-functional.* The advertisement has become memorable as well as easy to convey and receive, as a result of such a rich lexical inventory.

b. Advertisement made by ChatGPT 3.5
Prompt: *Please write a short description for the Face Reality toner for the website advertisement. Please select and use some linguistic measures from semantic/syntactic/rhetorical level. Below the description, please indicate what types of linguistic measures you used and what is their objective in this advertisement.*

BOX 5.32   FACE REALITY, TONER – ADVERTISEMENT BY CHATGPT 3.5

Introducing Face Reality Clarifying Toner: Your Solution to Clear, Balanced Skin
   Achieve clearer, healthier skin with Face Reality Clarifying Toner. Formulated with potent botanical extracts and gentle acids, this toner effectively reduces excess oil, minimizes pores, and prevents breakouts without drying out your skin. Perfect for daily use, it balances your skin's pH levels, leaving it refreshed and radiant.

Linguistic measures used:

Semantic level:

- Positive adjectives: "Clearer", "healthier", "effective", "gentle", "refreshed", "radiant".
- Domain-specific terms: "Botanical extracts", "gentle acids", "balances pH levels", "minimizes pores". These terms establish the toner's efficacy and suitability for skincare needs.
- Ethical appeal: Emphasising gentle ingredients and effectiveness without harsh chemicals appeals to consumers seeking natural and safe skincare solutions.

Syntactic level:

- Complex sentence: "Formulated with potent botanical extracts and gentle acids, this toner effectively reduces excess oil, minimizes pores, and prevents breakouts without drying out your skin." This structure combines related information to showcase multiple benefits.
- Imperative sentence: "Achieve clearer, healthier skin with Face Reality Clarifying Toner." This encourages immediate action from potential customers.

Rhetorical level:

- Metaphor: "Your Solution to Clear, Balanced Skin" suggests the toner as a remedy for achieving balanced and clear skin, enhancing its appeal.
- Alliteration: "Formulated with potent botanical extracts" creates a pleasing rhythm and emphasises the natural ingredients' potency.
- Direct address: "Perfect for daily use" directly addresses the consumer, highlighting convenience and practicality.

Objectives:

Semantic level: The positive adjectives and domain-specific terms aim to convey the toner's effectiveness, gentle formulation, and beneficial properties for skin health.

Syntactic level: Complex sentences provide detailed information and benefits, while imperative sentences prompt immediate interest and action from potential customers.

Rhetorical level: Metaphor and alliteration enhance the toner's appeal and memorability, while direct address emphasises its suitability for daily skincare routines, appealing to consumers seeking clear, balanced skin without harsh chemicals.

ChatGPT 3.5 generated a half-correct advertisement, as it was certainly not without errors. On the one hand, on a semantic level, the incorrectly identified linguistic measure is the ethical appeal, which is not a linguistic measure but could make a very good objective. On the other hand, positive adjectives and domain-specific terms, which represent a conveyance inducing the purchase of a product, were correctly listed. Furthermore, there were two *clearer* and *healthier* positive adjectives, which are also the comparative degree that suggests the product is the best of its kind without disparaging others.

The syntactic level was semi-well managed by ChatGPT. The linguistic measures enumerated by it are complex and imperative sentences. While the second linguistic measure is well and aptly presented, it differs from the first. As mentioned earlier, complex sentences are highly undesirable in advertisements because of their intricacy. They negatively affect the persuasive message. Moreover, the sentence – *Achieve clearer, healthier skin with Face Reality Clarifying Toner* – is worth mentioning as being the only short sentence in this advertisement and performing a persuasive function through ease of perception.

On a rhetorical level, only the metaphor is correctly identified and discussed. Once again, though, there are alliteration mistakes, as there are no repeated sounds in the phrase *formulated with potent botanical extracts* by any means. ChatGPT could have accurately identified the alliteration if it had substituted the words *refreshed* and *radiant*, where the consonant "r" is genuinely repeated. In addition, direct address was misused, as the phrase *perfect for daily use* may be inviting, but it does not directly address the consumer.

As far as the objectives are concerned, there were different results. Certainly, the well-positioned objectives are those at the semantic level. At the syntactic level, objectives were only correctly applied to the imperative sentence. On the rhetorical level, by contrast, objectives should only refer to the metaphor, which occurred in the list of linguistic measures used.

c. Advertisement made by ChatGPT 4.0

BOX 5.33   FACE REALITY, TONER – ADVERTISEMENT BY CHATGPT 4.0

Transform your skincare routine with Face Reality Toner. This gentle yet effective toner clarifies and balances your skin, leaving it impeccably clean and refreshed. Infused with soothing ingredients, it works harmoniously to minimize pores and enhance your skin's natural glow. Perfect for daily use, this toner will guide your skin back to its optimal state of clear, calm beauty. Embrace a new reality – where flawless skin is your everyday truth.

Linguistic measures used:

1. Metaphor (rhetorical level): The phrase "Embrace a new reality" uses a metaphor that suggests the product can alter the user's skincare experience significantly, implying a transformative effect that leads to a new state of being for the skin.

2. Alliteration (rhetorical level): "Clear, calm beauty" uses alliteration with the repetition of the "c" sound, enhancing the auditory appeal of the text and making the benefits sound more poetic and attractive.

3. Imperative sentence (syntactic level): "Embrace a new reality" is an imperative sentence that encourages the reader to accept and engage with the transformative potential of the toner. It directly engages the reader, prompting action.

4. Positive adjectives (lexical level): Descriptors like "gentle", "effective", "soothing", and "flawless" positively characterise the toner, highlighting its benefits and appealing directly to the consumer's desire for effective and nurturing skincare products.

5. Parallelism (rhetorical level): The construction "clarifies and balances your skin, leaving it impeccably clean and refreshed" employs parallel structure to emphasise the comprehensive benefits of the toner in a balanced and rhythmic manner, making the description more persuasive and memorable.

ChatGPT 4.0, in comparison to its earlier version, amazed and generated a much more improved advertisement, rich in linguistic measures. It is reasonable to assume that by the number of linguistic measures used, the advertisement has a strong persuasive effect.

Noteworthy is the finding that AI identified as many as 80% of them correctly. The following were successfully summarised:

1. The metaphor *embrace a new reality* with the proper objective. Due to the suggested "transformative effect", the advertising message can be persuasive or even manipulative.

2. The alliteration appeared in the phrase <u>c</u>lear, <u>c</u>alm beauty with the "c" sound repeated. The alliteration and its objective were also correctly presented.

3. Once again, the phrase *embrace a new reality* appears, but this time at the syntactic level as the imperative sentence, which naturally corresponds to the reality. One can also find another sentence not mentioned by ChatGPT 4.0, namely *transform your skincare.* Imperatives prompt action, and so it happens in this case.

4. Positive adjectives listed are *gentle, effective, soothing,* and *flawless.* In fact, these are only four of them. There are actually more to be found, as ChatGPT has used as many as 11 favourable adjectives. In addition to those just mentioned, these are *clean, refreshed, natural, perfect, optimal, clear,* and *calm.*

Moreover, unfortunately, ChatGPT failed to adequately apply and detect parallel structures. The construction "clarifies and balances your skin, leaving it impeccably clean and refreshed" is not parallelism, as the grammatical structure is not repeated.

Other than the listed linguistic measures by AI, the personal pronoun *your* can also be identified, which is repeated as many as five times. Additionally, on a syntactic level, the first opening sentence of the advertisement (*Transform your skincare routine with Face Reality Toner*) is also simple and short. Combined with the imperative function, it creates a sentence that non-literally strikes the consumer with its persuasiveness.

With all of this in mind, despite one minor error, the above-mentioned advertisement is abundant on all linguistic levels. ChatGPT version 4.0 correctly handled the identification and listed a significant number of the measures used. Furthermore, the ending sentence of the advertisement, *embrace a new reality – where flawless skin is your everyday truth*, is worth noting, creating a sensational slogan that will definitely encourage the purchase and be remembered by many consumers.

Example 7

a. Advertisement made by a human

> ### BOX 5.34   AVON, SHAMPOO – ADVERTISEMENT BY A HUMAN
>
> *If you think it's just your skin that needs hydration, think again! Did you know that water makes up 25% of our hair, but sun, styling and heat can dehydrate it, resulting in lacklustre, lifeless stands? But with our Advance Techniques Hydra Boost Shampoo, you can treat your hair like you would your skin, with weightless hydration that revives lifeless locks and dehydrated scalps.*

In the above-mentioned example, the most important tempting element is the order and the sequence of sentences used at the syntactic level. The first sentence (*If you think it's just your skin that needs hydration, think again!*) is imperative and gives a command to think and reconsider the statement. A sentence that follows (*Did you know that water makes up 25% of our hair, but sun, styling and heat can dehydrate it, resulting in lacklustre, lifeless stands?*) is interrogative and manipulates the consumer's mindset. When the consumer has directed his thinking according to the plan, the advertiser gives the solution in the last sentence (*But with our Advance Techniques Hydra Boost Shampoo, you can treat your hair like you would your skin, with weightless hydration that revives lifeless locks and dehydrated scalps).* A simple but a very effective method.

The advertisement does not have any rhetorical features but it does the lexical ones. For instance, it makes use of monosyllabic verbs such as *think, know, makes, treat,* and *like.* They create the advertisement easier to understand. It also elicits negative adjectives like *lacklustre, lifeless,* and *dehydrated* to stimulate the imagination and draw attention to the problem. The commercial contains personal pronouns (*you, your, our*) to make it more individualised.

b. Advertisement made by ChatGPT 3.5
Prompt: *Please write a short description for the Avon Advance Techniques Hydra Boost Shampoo for the website advertisement. Please select and use some linguistic measures from semantic/syntactic/rhetorical level. Below the description, please indicate what types of linguistic measures you used and what is their objective in this advertisement.*

BOX 5.35   AVON, SHAMPOO – ADVERTISEMENT BY CHATGPT 3.5

Introducing Avon Advance Techniques Hydra Boost Shampoo: Hydration and Shine in Every Wash
   Transform your hair care routine with Avon Advance Techniques Hydra Boost Shampoo. Infused with hyaluronic acid and provitamin B5, this luxurious shampoo replenishes moisture, leaving hair hydrated, silky-smooth, and beautifully shiny. Perfect for all hair types, it gently cleanses without weighing hair down, revealing nourished locks from root to tip.

Linguistic measures used:

Semantic level:

• Positive adjectives: "Hydrated", "silky-smooth", "beautifully shiny", "nourished".
• Specific ingredients: "Hyaluronic acid", "provitamin B5". These highlight key components known for their moisturising and nourishing properties, appealing to consumers concerned with hair health.

Syntactic level:

- Compound sentences: "Infused with hyaluronic acid and provitamin B5, this luxurious shampoo replenishes moisture, leaving hair hydrated, silky-smooth, and beautifully shiny." This structure links ingredients to benefits, showcasing the shampoo's efficacy.
- Descriptive phrases: "Perfect for all hair types", "gently cleanses without weighing hair down". These phrases provide clarity about the shampoo's versatility and performance.

Rhetorical level:

- Imagery: "Transform your hair care routine" evokes a sense of positive change and improvement in hair health.
- Alliteration: "Hydration and Shine in Every Wash" creates a rhythmic quality and emphasises the dual benefits of moisture and shine.
- Direct address: "Perfect for all hair types" directly addresses the consumer's needs, promoting inclusivity and broad appeal.

Objectives:

Semantic level: The use of positive adjectives and specific ingredients aims to convey the shampoo's effectiveness in hydrating, smoothing, and enhancing hair shine.

Syntactic level: Compound sentences and descriptive phrases provide detailed information about the shampoo's benefits and suitability for all hair types, promoting its versatility and performance.

Rhetorical level: Imagery and alliteration enhance the shampoo's appeal and memorability, while direct address emphasises its broad applicability, appealing to consumers seeking a luxurious yet effective hair care solution.

The above-mentioned advertisement generated by ChatGPT 3.5 is rather average in terms of persuasiveness or manipulation. Moreover, AI puts a great deal of misidentification, both in linguistic measures and in objectives.

Starting at the very beginning of the list proposed by ChatGPT – on a semantic level, positive adjectives are adequately represented, as are their later objectives. Moreover, the adjective *silky-smooth also* functions as a compound. The use of specific ingredients is not a linguistic measure. In addition, the weasel word – *transform* – and the personal pronoun – *your* – are also present at this level but not identified.

Regarding the syntactic level, it was properly identified, while being undesirable in advertisements by its complexity. Compound sentences and descriptive phrases are overly elaborate, so their reception can be difficult or even incomprehensible for an individual.

On a rhetorical level, all linguistic measures have been misidentified; moreover, the advertisement does not have any other measures that can be undetected by ChatGPT. First of all, imagery is the use of figurative language to evoke a feeling, and the phrase *transform your hair care routine* does not use figurative language; therefore, it excludes the use of that linguistic measure. The following phrase is more suited to the previously mentioned weasel word. Furthermore, on a rhetorical level, the alliteration is again misidentified as the sounds are not repeated after each other in any manner. Direct address is also a poorly chosen linguistic measure.

Altogether, this advertisement has rather little to do with persuasion or manipulation. ChatGPT failed to correctly identify most of the linguistic measures. Regarding the objectives, only one was correctly set, namely on the semantic level. Objectives from the syntactic level are completely misrepresented, as the previously mentioned linguistic measures have a negative effect on advertisement. As for the objectives from the rhetorical level, they cannot be correct due to incorrect linguistic measures.

c. Advertisement made by ChatGPT 4.0

**BOX 5.36   AVON, SHAMPOO – ADVERTISEMENT
BY CHATGPT 4.0**

Quench your hair's thirst with Avon Advance Techniques Hydra Boost Shampoo. Infused with nutrient-rich ingredients, this shampoo delivers a surge of hydration to every strand, revitalizing dry and lifeless hair. Experience the rejuvenation as your locks absorb the moisture, transforming into silky, glossy tresses. Embrace the vitality of deeply nourished hair – shine with every wash.

Linguistic measures used:

1. Metaphor (rhetorical level): "Quench your hair's thirst" uses a metaphor that personifies hair as being thirsty, enhancing the perception that this shampoo is as essential as water for dry hair, which emphasises its hydrating qualities.

2. Alliteration (rhetorical level): The phrase "silky, glossy tresses" employs alliteration with the repetition of the "s" sound, creating a smooth and pleasing auditory effect that makes the product benefits memorable and attractive.

3. Imperative sentence (syntactic level): "Embrace the vitality of deeply nourished hair" is an imperative sentence that not only instructs but also inspires the consumer to experience the benefits of the product, encouraging them to feel the transformation.

4. Positive adjectives (lexical level): Adjectives like "nutrient-rich", "hydrating", "rejuvenating", and "vitality" positively enhance the description, emphasising the product's effectiveness and appealing to consumers looking for solutions to specific hair care needs.

5. Parallelism (rhetorical level): "Experience the rejuvenation as your locks absorb the moisture, transforming into silky, glossy tresses" uses parallel structure to balance the sentence, enhancing readability, and emphasising the dual benefits of moisture absorption and transformation.

When it comes to the Avon shampoo advertisement proposed by ChatGPT 4.0, there are hardly any errors in it, and it also uses language measures at all levels. The following are the linguistic measures listed by ChatGPT:

1. The metaphor *quench your hair's thirst* is both advanced and engaging. It definitely encourages purchase as it implies that our hair will no longer be thirsty after using the shampoo, that is, it will leave it sufficiently moisturised, which fits perfectly with the name of the shampoo *Hydra Boost.*

2. The alliteration does not occur in this advertisement through the repetition of the "s" sound in *silky, glossy tresses*, but it has a very well explained objective.

3. Imperative sentence at the syntactic level is also correctly identified together with the objective.

4. Positive (favourable) adjectives, i.e. *nutrient-rich, hydrating, rejuvenating*, were correctly distinguished and identified by the AI. Unfortunately, this point also included one word that is not an adjective but a noun, namely *vitality*. As for the above-mentioned adjectives, it can also be added that *nutrient-rich* is a compound.

5. Parallelism does appear in that advertisement but not in this particular example provided by ChatGPT. Chat states that the parallel structure is the sentence *Experience the rejuvenation as your locks absorb the moisture, transforming into silky, glossy tresses*; however, as mentioned earlier, it does not function as a parallel structure alone. It can, nevertheless, do so in combination with the sentence occurring after it. Namely, both sentences have the same grammatical construction applied at the beginning, which is shown by underlining:

a) *Experience the rejuvenation as your locks absorb the moisture, transforming into silky, glossy tresses.*

b) *Embrace the vitality of deeply nourished hair-shine with every wash.*

In summary, this is a highly persuasive advertisement; thus, it used linguistic measures on all possible levels. Despite minor errors in identification by ChatGPT 4.0, the objectives were retained and most of the linguistic measures were correctly quoted and matched to the appropriate levels.

5.3 CONCLUSIONS TO THE ANALYSIS

First of all, conclusions to human-made advertisements will be presented. The findings indicate that the authors of selected beauty products advertising messages masterfully employ tactics for influencing our perceptions and emotions. Advertising can be called a game played between the sender and the receiver. The advertiser speaks the consumer's language and identifies with their needs. The outcomes of the research were pattered and presented in the following table:

BOX 5.37   THE USE OF PARTICULAR LINGUISTIC FEATURES

| | | LINGUISTIC FEATURES USED | | |
	EXAMPLE	AT THE LEXICAL LEVEL	AT THE SYNTACTIC LEVEL	AT THE RHETORICAL LEVEL
Make-up products	1	+	-	+
	2	+	+	+
	3	+	-	+
	4	+	+	+
	5	+	+	+
Skin/body/hair care products	1	+	+	+
	2	+	-	+
	3	+	+	+
	4	+	-	+
	5	+	+	+
	6	+	+	-
	7	+	+	-

The box above shows the occurrence of linguistic features at specific levels. The sign "+" means that there were language tools used in the advertisement at a particular level, and the sign "-" means they did not appear. It can be deduced that linguistic features at the lexical level were employed in all advertisements analysed (12+). Then, many were used at the rhetorical level (10+) and the least at the syntactical level (8+). Although the most frequently used language features by advertisements were at the lexical level, at the syntactical and rhetorical levels were also common. Due to the fact that all of the provided advertisements were highly persuasive, it can be concluded that the number of language features leads to a more effective persuasion and manipulation. Furthermore, when it came to human-made advertisements, they were very diverse in the language measures they used, and each advertisement had something unique that made it stand out from the rest. The situation was different for the ChatGPT-generated advertisements, which will be discussed in the following.

Firstly, the advertisements generated by ChatGPT, in both versions 3.5 and 4.0, exhibited a highly schematic and repetitive nature. The linguistic features most frequently employed were favourable adjectives and imperative sentences, which appeared in nearly every advertisement. This repetition suggests a reliance on a limited set of persuasive tools, potentially diminishing the overall effectiveness and appeal of the advertisements. Additionally, all the advertisements displayed a high level of syntactic complexity, characterised by intricate sentence structures. While simple, short, or minor sentences were present, they were relatively rare. This syntactic complexity can detract from the persuasive efficacy of the advertisements, as they may become difficult for the average consumer to comprehend and engage with.

Moreover, a clear distinction was observed between the advertisements produced by ChatGPT versions 3.5 and 4.0. Version 3.5 tended to produce less sophisticated advertisements, relying more heavily on basic linguistic features and repetitive patterns. In contrast, version 4.0 incorporated a wider variety of more interesting linguistic features, resulting in advertisements that were not only more engaging but also presented a more coherent and polished overall message. This suggests that advancements in the AI's capabilities have led to improvements in the quality and effectiveness of the generated content.

However, despite these improvements, both versions of ChatGPT exhibited difficulties in accurately identifying and utilising linguistic features. Misidentification of linguistic elements was common, for instance, with features such as alliteration, which were either incorrectly identified or omitted altogether. These omissions are significant, as such features can greatly enhance the persuasive power of an advertisement. Furthermore, while ChatGPT 4.0 showed some ability to correctly classify linguistic features into lexical, syntactic, or rhetorical levels, this was not consistently achieved. ChatGPT 3.5, in particular, failed to match linguistic features to the appropriate levels, indicating a gap in its linguistic analytical capabilities.

In spite of these challenges, artificial intelligence, as demonstrated by ChatGPT, excelled in articulating and explaining objectives comprehensively. The AI's ability to clearly outline the goals of an advertisement and provide detailed explanations of its components is noteworthy. However, it was occasionally evident that not all outlined objectives were inherently persuasive. Some linguistic features appeared to be included merely to create a perception of complexity, rather than to enhance the persuasive impact of the message.

In summary, the strengths of human-crafted advertisements lie in their innovation, diversity, and meticulous planning. The authors of these advertisements displayed a understanding of how to strategically deploy specific linguistic measures to enhance persuasive content. Their approach not only maximised the impact of the messages but also demonstrated a rich and varied use of language. This diversity in linguistic strategies allowed human advertisers to tailor their messages in ways that deeply resonate with the target audience, showcasing a nuanced and deliberate crafting process.

On the other hand, ChatGPT exhibited remarkable proficiency in the lexical domain when creating advertisements. The artificial intelligence's ability to access and utilise a vast range of vocabulary enabled it to construct compelling and articulate messages. This lexical strength highlights one of the key advantages of AI in advertising – the ability to generate a wide array of language options quickly and efficiently. By leveraging this extensive vocabulary, ChatGPT can serve as a valuable tool for human advertisers, providing inspiration and expanding the creative possibilities for crafting persuasive content.

Thus, while human advertisers excel in the strategic and diverse application of linguistic techniques, artificial intelligence stands out for its lexical richness and ability to generate language options. The interplay between human creativity and AI capabilities can potentially lead to even more effective and innovative advertising strategies, combining the best of both worlds to influence and engage consumers more profoundly.

NOTES

1. Retrieved July 22, 2024, from https://www.collinsdictionary.com/dictionary/english/to-speak-volumes.
2. Retrieved July 22, 2024, from https://www.collinsdictionary.com/dictionary/english/soiree.
3. Retrieved June 14, 2022, from https://www.merriam-webster.com/thesaurus/antidote.
4. Retrieved July 22, 2024, from https://www.collinsdictionary.com/dictionary/english/linger.
5. Retrieved June 14, 2022, from https://www.merriam-webster.com/dictionary/hangry.
6. Retrieved June 14, 2022, from https://idioms.thefreedictionary.com/a+feast+for+the+eyes.

Conclusions

The exploration of advertising within this book underlines its profound impact on consumer culture. Advertising's ability to shape perceptions and influence behaviour hinges significantly on the sophisticated use of language. The theoretical framework laid out in the initial chapters provides a comprehensive understanding of advertising's complex nature. From its definition and major functions to the nuanced distinction between persuasion and manipulation, the book meticulously dissects the components that make advertising a powerful tool for marketers.

The in-depth analysis of linguistic features used in advertising reveals how language operates at multiple levels – lexical, syntactic, and rhetorical – to captivate and persuade audiences. Lexical features such as monosyllabic verbs, weasel words, and favourable adjectives create clear, impactful messages. Syntactic features like imperative and interrogative sentences, alongside short and simple structures, enhance readability and engagement. Rhetorical devices including metaphors, personification, similes, and puns add a layer of creativity and emotional appeal, making advertisements memorable and compelling.

The third and fourth chapters analyse the transformative role of artificial intelligence (AI) in management, marketing, and specifically advertising. AI's integration into these domains has transformed traditional practices, introducing advanced data-driven decision-making tools and generative capabilities. ChatGPT, as an example of generative AI, demonstrates both the potential and the limitations of AI in creating persuasive advertisements. While AI can generate articulate and diverse language quickly, it often lacks the nuanced creativity and strategic depth that human advertisers bring to their work.

The comparative analysis between human-generated and ChatGPT-generated advertisements offers insightful revelations. Human advertisements are characterised by their innovative and strategic use of language, creating messages that deeply resonate with the target audience. In contrast, AI-generated advertisements, though rich in vocabulary and articulate in presentation, tend to be repetitive and schematic. The improvements seen in ChatGPT version 4.0 over version 3.5 highlight the ongoing advancements in AI capabilities, yet also emphasise the persistent gap in creativity and strategic application compared to human efforts.

The findings suggest a promising future where human creativity and AI efficiency can be synergistically combined. Human advertisers can use AI's extensive lexical resources and rapid generation capabilities to enhance their creative processes. This collaboration can lead to the development of more innovative, engaging, and persuasive advertising content. The book advocates for a balanced approach, where AI serves as a powerful tool improving human creativity rather than replacing it.

The ethical implications of AI in advertising, discussed in the fourth chapter, are highly important. As AI becomes more integrated into advertising practices, concerns about transparency, manipulation, and consumer privacy must be addressed. Ethical guidelines and regulations will be essential to ensure that AI is used responsibly, maintaining consumer trust and safeguarding against manipulative practices.

In conclusion, this book provides a thorough analysis of the language of advertising, the transformative role of AI, and the comparative effectiveness of human versus AI-generated content. The observations gleaned from this study highlight the enduring importance of human creativity in advertising, even as AI continues to evolve and offer new possibilities. The future of advertising lies in the collaborative integration of human ingenuity with AI's generative capabilities, promising a new era of innovative and impactful advertising strategies.

Summary

Advertising is an inherent part of modern consumer culture. The aim of this work is to investigate the advertisement's language functions and shows advertisements as persuasive and manipulative tools. The book deals with linguistic analysis of beauty products advertisements made by a human, by ChatGPT 3.5, and by ChatGPT 4.0 and claims that the language tools used in advertising have a significant impact on its message.

Chapter 1 demonstrates that advertising is a fundamental form of communication and its purpose is to inform and persuade consumers. Its most important functions are listed, i.e. attention value, readability, memorability, and selling power. Then persuasion was separated from manipulation. Persuasion techniques are given as well as the phenomenon of implicature and presupposition.

Chapter 2 proves that the language of advertising is a language for specific purposes and discusses its linguistic features at three levels – lexical, syntactic, and rhetorical, respectively. Lexical level refers to the selected lexical items that are applicable in the advertisement. Items such as monosyllabic verbs, weasel words, favourable words, personal pronouns, compounds, and neologisms are discussed. At the syntactical level, sentences that appear in advertisements are considered – imperative, interrogative, short, simple, and minor. Rhetoric level refers to items that are used to enhance the power of language such as metaphor, personification, simile, alliteration, hyperbole, euphemism, parallelism, and punning.

Chapter 3 explores AI's role in management, marketing, and advertising. It deals with specific applications of AI in these domains, highlighting how AI technologies are being integrated to enhance efficiency and effectiveness.

Chapter 4 focuses on generative AI and its impact on advertising. It examines the capabilities of ChatGPT, detailing its features and discussing the ethical considerations surrounding its use. This chapter demonstrates the way generative AI tools like ChatGPT are transforming advertising strategies and practices.

Chapter 5 provides a comparative analysis of advertisements for beauty products created by humans, ChatGPT 3.5, and ChatGPT 4.0. This analysis includes make-up and skin/body/hair care products, examining the differences in language and persuasiveness. Initially, advertisements created by humans are analysed based on linguistic measures used and their persuasiveness.

Subsequently, both versions of ChatGPT are asked to create advertisements, enumerate the linguistic measures used, and describe them. The advertisements crafted by ChatGPT 3.5 and 4.0 are then analysed and evaluated to determine if these AI models accurately recognised and used these measures. The findings aim to demonstrate the strengths and weaknesses of human versus AI-generated advertisements in terms of linguistic features and their effectiveness.

This book seeks to offer a thorough understanding of advertising language and the growing influence of AI in this domain, delivering valuable information for researchers, marketers, and AI developers.

References

Adiwardana, D., Luong, M.-T., So, D. R., Hall, J., Fiedel, N., Thoppilan, R. Yang, Z. Kulshreshtha, A. Nemade, G., Lu, Y., & Quoc, V. L. (2020). Towards a human-like open-domain chatbot. *arXiv preprint.* arXiv:2001.09977.

Alani, E.; Kamarudin, S.; Alrubaiee, L., & Tavakoli, R. (2019). A model of the relationship between strategic orientation and product innovation under the mediating effect of customer knowledge management. *J. Int. Stud, 12,* 232–242.

Algeo, J. (2014). Fifty years among the new words: A dictionary of neologisms 1941–1991. Cambridge University Press.

Alghamdi, O. A., & Agag, G. (2023). Boosting innovation performance through big data analytics pow- ered by artificial intelligence use: An empirical exploration of the role of strategic agility and mar- ket turbulence. *Sustainability, 15(19),* 14296.

Alhashmi, S. F. S., Salloum, S. A., & Abdallah, S. (2019). Critical success factors for implementing Artificial Intelligence (AI) projects in Dubai Government United Arab Emirates (UAE) health sector: Applying the extended Technology Acceptance Model (TAM). In *International Conference on Advanced Intelligent Systems and Informatics* (pp. 1–12). Springer.

Allam, Z., & Jones, D. S. (2021). Future (post-COVID) digital, smart and sustainable cities in the wake of 6G: Digital twins, immersive realities and new urban economies. *Land Use Policy, 101,* 105201.

Allamanis, M., Barr, E. T., Devanbu, P., & Sutton, C. (2018). A survey of machine learning for big code and naturalness. *ACM Computing Surveys (CSUR), 51(4),* 81.

Ameen, N., Tarhini, A., Reppel, A., & Anand, A. (2021). Customer experiences in the age of artificial intelligence. *Computers in Human Behavior, 114,* 106548. https://doi.org/10.1016/j.chb.2020.106548

Andonians, V. (2023). Harnessing hybrid intelligence: Balancing AI models and human expertise for optimal performance. *Datanami.* https://www.datanami.com/2023/04/11/harnessing-hybrid-intelligence-balancing-ai-models-and-human-expertise-for-optimal-performance-2/

Appelbaum, D., Kogan, A., & Vasarhelyi, M. A. (2017). Big data and analytics in the modern audit engagement: Research needs. *Auditing A Journal of Practice & Theory, 36,* 1–27. https://doi.org/10.2308/ajpt-51684

Arntz, M., Gregory, T., & Zierahn, U. (2016). The risk of automation for jobs in OECD countries: A comparative analysis. *OECD Social, Employment, and Migration Working Papers, 189,* 34. https://jyu.finna.fi/PrimoRecord/pci.proquest1790436902

Árvay, A. (2004). Pragmatic aspects of persuasion and manipulation in written advertisements. *Acta Linguistica Hungarica, 51,* 231–263. https://doi.org/10.1556/aling.51.2004.3-4.2

Autor, D. H. (2015). Why are there still so many jobs? The history and future of workplace automation. *The Journal of Economic Perspectives, 29*(3), 3–30. https://doi.org/10.1257/jep.29.3.3

Ayers, J. W., Poliak, A., Dredze, M., Leas, E. C., Zhu, Z., Kelley, J. B., Faix, D. J., Goodman, A. M., Longhurst, C. A., Hogarth, M., & Smith, D. M. (2023). Comparing physician and artificial intelligence chatbot responses to patient questions posted to a public social media forum. *JAMA Internal Medicine, 183*, 589–596.

Bahdanau, D., Cho, K., & Bengio, Y. (2015). Neural machine translation by jointly learning to align and translate. In *Proceedings of the 3rd International Conference on Learning Representations, ICLR 2015*, San Diego, CA, USA, May 7–9, 2015, Conference Track Proceedings.

Bang, Y., Cahyawijaya, S., Lee, N., et al. (2023). A multitask, multilingual, multimodal evaluation of ChatGPT on reasoning, hallucination, and interactivity. *arXiv preprint arXiv:2302.04023*. https://arxiv.org/abs/2302.04023

Barnali, C. (2015). Rhetorical devices in English advertisement texts in India: A descriptive study. *International Journal of Social Science and Humanity, 5*, 980–984. https://doi.org/10.7763/IJSSH.2015.V5.591

Berthon, P., Yalcin, T., Pehlivan, E., & Rabinovich, T. (2024). Trajectories of AI technologies: Insights for managers. *Business Horizons, 67*(5), 461–470.

Bhatt, V. K. (2021, November 24–26). *Assessing the significance and impact of artificial intelligence and machine learning in placement of advertisements* [Conference session]. 2021 IEEE International Conference on Technology Management, Operations and Decisions (ICTMOD), Marrakech, Morocco (pp. 1–6). IEEE.

Botha, J., & Pieterse, H. (2020, March). Fake news and deepfakes: A dangerous threat for 21st century information security. In *ICCWS 2020 15th International Conference on Cyber Warfare and Security*. Academic Conferences and Publishing Limited. https://researchspace.csir.co.za/dspace/handle/10204/11946

Braga, A.; Logan, R. K. (2017). The emperor of strong AI has no clothes: Limits to Artificial Intelligence. *Information, 8*, 156. https://doi.org/10.3390/info8040156

Bralczyk, J. (2004). *Język na sprzedaż*. Gdańskie Wydawnictwo Psychologiczne. ISBN: 83-89574-48-9

Brown, T. B., Mann, B., Ryder, N., Subbiah, M., Kaplan, J., Dhariwal, P., & Amodei, D. (2020). Language models are few-shot learners. *arXiv preprint arXiv:2005.14165*. https://arxiv.org/abs/2005.14165

Brynjolfsson, E., Li, D., & Raymond, L. R. (2023). Generative AI at work. *NBER Working Papers 31161*. National Bureau of Economic Research, Inc.

Brynjolfsson, E., & Mitchell, T.M. (2017). What can machine learning do? Workforce implications. *Science, 358*, 1530–1534.

Bubeck, S., et al. (2023). Sparks of artificial general intelligence: Early experiments with GPT-4. *arXiv preprint arXiv:2303.12712*. https://arxiv.org/abs/2303.12712

Budzyński, W. (2007). *Reklama: Techniki skutecznej perswazji*. Poltext. ISBN: 8386890622

Campbell, C., Plangger, K., Sands, S., & Kietzmann, J. (2022). Preparing for an era of deepfakes and AI-generated ads: A framework for understanding responses to manipulated advertising. *Journal of Advertising, 51*(1), 22–38.

Cao, M. (2021). Design and implementation of multidimensional interaction in online English course under the assistance of omnimedia. *Scientific Programming, 2021*, 1–10.

Castelo, N., Bos, M. W., & Lehmann, D. R. (2019). Task-dependent algorithm aversion. *Journal of Marketing Research, 56*(5), 809–825.

Cellerin, T. (2023, March 22). How ChatGPT is already disrupting the advertising industry. *LinkedIn.* https://www.linkedin.com/pulse/how-chatgpt-already-disrupting-advertising-industry-thierry-cellerin/

Chen, J.-S., Le, T.-T.-Y., & Florence, D. (2021). Usability and responsiveness of artificial intelligence chatbot on online customer experience in e-retailing. *International Journal of Retail & Distribution Management, 49*(11), 1512–1531. https://doi.org/10.1108/IJRDM-08-2020-0312

Chen, Q., Zeng, L., & Zhang, Q. (2020). Deep learning for quantitative finance: A survey. *IEEE Transactions on Knowledge and Data Engineering, 34*, 3800–3813.

Chen, Z., Liu, B. (2018). *Lifelong machine learning.* Springer.

Cieciura, P. (2009). Reklama a style funkcjonalne języka. Zarys problematyki. *Bohemistyka, 3*, 204–212.

Clayton, J. (2023, May 16). Sam Altman: CEO of OpenAI calls for US to regulate artificial intelligence. *BBC News.* https://www.bbc.com/news/world-us-canada-65616866

Clugston, R. (2023, May 4). Why ChatGPT and AI can't make world-changing, transformative work. *Adhesives Age.* https://adage.com/article/opinion/why-chatgpt-and-ai-cant-make-world-changing-transformative-work/2491856

Corbo, L., Costa, S., & Dabi, M. (2022). The evolving role of artificial intelligence in marketing: A review and research agenda. *Journal of Business Research, 128*(March 2020), 187–203.

Cooke, P., Leydesdorff, L. (2006). Regional development in the knowledge-based economy: The construction of advantage. *J Technol Transfer, 31*, 5–15. https://doi.org/10.1007/s10961-005-5009-3

Crystal, D. (2008). *A dictionary of linguistics and phonetics.* Blackwell Publishing. ISBN: 978-1-405-15296-9

Culler, J. (2005). *On puns: The foundation of letters.* Internet-First University Press. ISBN: 0-631-15893-6

Dalamu, T. O. (2018). Euphemism: The commonplace of advertising culture. *Acta Scientiarum. Language and Culture, 40*, 1–15. https://doi.org/10.4025/actasci-langcult.v40i2.41107

Danciu, V. (2014). Manipulative marketing: persuasion and manipulation of the consumer through advertising. *Theoretical and Applied Economics, 21*, 19–34.

Daqar, M. A. A., & Smoudy, A. K. (2019). The role of artificial intelligence on enhancing customer experience. *International Review of Management and Marketing, 9*(4), 22.

Davenport, T. H., Guha, A., Grewal, D., & Bressgott, T. (2020). How artificial intelligence will change the future of marketing. *Journal of the Academy of Marketing Science, 48*(1), 24–42.

Davenport, T. H. & Mittal, N. (2023). How companies can prepare for the coming "AI-first" world. *Strategy & Leadership, 51*(1), 26–30. https://doi.org/10.1108/SL-11-2022-0107

Davenport, T. H., & Ronanki, R. (2018). Artificial intelligence for the real world. *Harvard Business Review, 96*(1), 108–116.

De Mauro, A., Sestino, A., & Bacconi, A. (2022). Machine learning and artificial intelligence use in marketing: A general taxonomy. *Italian Journal of Marketing, 2022*, 439–457. https://doi.org/10.1007/s43039-022-00057-w

Dermawan, E., & Barkah, C. (2022). Effective communication in advertising. *Jurnal Ekonomi, 16*, 148–155. https://doi.org/10.55208/jebe.v16i2.265

Dietvorst, B. J., Simmons, J. P., & Massey, C. (2015). Algorithm aversion: People erroneously avoid algorithms after seeing them. *Journal of Experimental Psychology: General, 144*(1), 114.

Díez-Arroyo, M. (2013). Scientific language in skin-care advertising: Persuading through opacity. *Revista Espanola de Linguistica Aplicada, 26*, 197–214.

Dimitrieska, S., Danevska, B. A., & Stanoevska, P. E. (2024). Brands in the metaverse. *Entrepreneurship, 6*(2018). https://doi.org/10.37708/ep.swu.v11i2.3

Dimitrieska, S., Stankovska, A., & Efremova, T. (2018). Artificial intelligence and marketing. *Entrepreneurship, 6*(2), 298–304.

Dumitriu, D., & Popescu, M. A. M. (2020). Artificial intelligence solutions for digital marketing. *Procedia Manufacturing, 46*, 630–636.

Dutton, K. (2010). *Flipnosis: The art of split-second persuasion.* William Heinemann. ISBN: 978-0434016914

EDPB. (2023). Report of the work undertaken by the ChatGPT taskforce. https://edpb.europa.eu/system/files/2023-07/edpb_2023_taskforce_report.pdf

Elbashir, M. Z., Collier, P. A., & Sutton, S. G. (2011). The role of organizational absorptive capacity in strategic use of business intelligence to support integrated management control systems. *The Accounting Review, 86*(1), 155–184.

Elgammal, A., Liu, B., Elhoseiny, M., & Mazzone, M. (2017). CAN: Creative adversarial networks, generating "art" by learning about styles and deviating from style norms. In A. Goel, A. Jordanous, & A. Pease (Eds.), *International Conference on Computational Creativity.* Georgia Institute of Technology.

Eloundou, T., et al. (2023). GPTs are GPTs: An early look at the labor market impact potential of large language models. *arXiv preprint arXiv:2303.10130.* https://arxiv.org/abs/2303.10130

Fajri, M. S. (2017). The Functions of Conversational Implicatures in Print Advertising. *Jurnal Pendidikan Bahasa dan Sastra, 17*, 1–15. https://doi.org/10.17509/bs_jpbsp.v17i1.6953

Fan, Y. (2013). The lexical features of English advertisement. *Advances in Intelligent Systems Research, 43*, 341–343. https://doi.org/10.2991/mdhss-13.2013.90

Ferraro, C., Demsar, V., Sands, S., Restrepo, M., & Campbell, C. (2024). The paradoxes of generative AI enabled customer service: A guide for managers. *Business Horizons, 67*(5), 549–559.

Fischer, S. (2023, May 30). Generative AI comes for advertising. *AXIOS.* https://www.axios.com/2023/05/30/generative-ai-comes-for-advertising

Fleming, P. (2019). Robots and organization studies: Why robots might not want to steal your job. *Organization Studies, 40*(1), 23–38.

Forrest, E., & Hoanca, B. (2015). Artificial intelligence: Marketing's game changer. In *Trends and innovations in marketing information systems* (pp. 45–64). https://doi.org/10.4018/978-1-4666-8459-1

Foster, A. T. (1988). Artificial intelligence in project management. *Cost Engineering, 30*(1), 21.

Fourcade, M., & Healy, K. (2016). Seeing like a market. *Socio-Economic Review, 15(1)*, 9–29.

Frey, C. B., & Osborne, M. A. (2013). The future of employment: How susceptible are jobs to computerisation? *Technological Forecasting and Social Change, 114*, 254–280.

Fridgeirsson, T. V., Ingason, H. T., Jonasson, H. I., & Jonsdottir, H. (2021). An authoritative study on the near future effect of artificial intelligence on project management knowledge areas. *Sustainability, 13*(4), 2345. https://doi.org/10.3390/su13042345

Fus, A. (2010). Język reklamy jako narzędzie perswazji i manipulacji na przykładzie wybranych polskich spotów telewizyjnych. *Investigationes Linguisticae, 19*, 53–62. https://doi.org/10.14746/il.2010.19.3

Gao, C., Lei, W., He, X., de Rijke, M., & Chua, T. S. (2021). Advances and challenges in conversational recommender systems: A survey. *AI Open, 2*, 100–126. https://doi.org/10.1016/j.aiopen.2021.02.003

Gebauer, H., Fleisch, E., Lamprecht, C., & Wortmann, F. (2020). Growth paths for overcoming the digitalization paradox. *Business Horizons, 63*(3), 313–323.

Ghimire, P., Kim, K., & Acharya, M. (2024). Opportunities and challenges of generative AI in construction industry: Focusing on adoption of text-based models. *Buildings, 14*(1), 220.

Gombolay, M. C., Gutierrez, R. A., Clarke, S. G., Sturla, G. F., & Shah, J. A. (2015). Decision-making authority, team efficiency and human worker satisfaction in mixed human–robot teams. *Autonomous Robots, 39*(3), 293–312. https://doi.org/10.1007/s10514-015-9457-9

Grand View Research. (2023). Generative AI market size to reach $109.37 billion by 2030. [Press release]. https://www.grandviewresearch.com/press-release/global-generative-ai-market

Gujar, P., & Panyam, S. (2024). Generative AI in digital advertising campaigns. *International Journal of Computer Trends and Technology, 72*(5), 51–55. https://doi.org/10.14445/22312803/IJCTT-V72I5P106

Gümüsay, A., Bohné, T., & Davenport, T. (2022). AI and the future of management decision-making. *Management and Business Review*, 1–19.

Guo, B., & Jiang, Z. (2023). Influence *of personalised advertising copy on consumer engagement: A field experiment approach.* Electronic Commerce Research. https://doi.org/10.1007/s10660-023-09721-5

Guo, S., Wang, Y., Li, S., & Saeed, N. (2023). Semantic communications with ordered importance using ChatGPT. *arXiv preprint arXiv:2302.07142.* https://arxiv.org/abs/2302.07142

Hacker, P., Engel, A., & Mauer, M. (2023). Regulating ChatGPT and other large generative AI models. In *Proceedings of the 2023 ACM Conference on Fairness, Accountability, and Transparency* (pp. 1112–1123).

Haenlein, M., & Kaplan, A. (2021). Artificial intelligence and robotics: Shaking up the business world and society at large. *Journal of Business Research, 124*, 405–407.

Haesevoets, T., De Cremer, D., Dierckx, K., & Van Hiel, A. (2021). Human-machine collaboration in managerial decision making. *Computers in Human Behavior, 119*. https://doi.org/10.1016/j.chb.2021.106730

Haleem, A., Javaid, M., Qadri, M. A., Suman, R. (2022). Understanding the role of digital technologies in education: A review. *Sustainable Operations and Computers, 3*, 275–285.

Hartmann, J., Schwenzow, J., & Witte, M. (2023). The political ideology of conversational AI: Converging evidence on ChatGPT's pro-environmental, left-libertarian orientation. *arXiv preprint arXiv:2301.01768.* https://arxiv.org/abs/2301.01768

Haupt, C. E., & Marks, M. (2023). AI-generated medical advice-GPT and beyond. *JAMA, 329*(16), 1349–1350. https://doi.org/10.1001/jama.2023.5321

Howarth, J. (2024). *55+ new generative AI stats.* Exploding Topics Blog. https://explodingtopics.com/blog/generative-ai-stats

Hu, K. (2023). ChatGPT sets record for fastest-growing user base. *Reuters.* https://www.reuters.com/technology/chatgpt-sets-record-fastest-growing-user-base-analyst-note-2023-02-01/

Huang, D. H., & Chueh, H. E. (2021). Chatbot usage intention analysis: Veterinary consultation. *Journal of Innovation & Knowledge, 2021*(6), 135–144. https://doi.org/10.1016/j.jik.2020.09.002

Huang, M. H., & Rust, R. T. (2018). Artificial intelligence in service. *Journal of Service Research, 21*(2), 155–172.

Huang, M.-H., & Rust, R. T. (2021). A strategic framework for artificial intelligence in marketing. *Journal of the Academy of Marketing Science, 49*(1), 30–50. https://doi.org/10.1007/s11747-020-00749-9

Huang, M.-H., & Rust, R. T. (2022). A framework for collaborative artificial intelligence in marketing. *Journal of Retailing, 98*(2), 209–223. https://doi.org/10.1016/j.jretai.2021.03.001

Jaiwant, S. V. (2023). The changing role of marketing: Industry 5.0-the game changer. In A. Saini & V. Garg (Eds.), *Transformation for sustainable business and management practices: Exploring the spectrum of industry 5.0* (pp. 187–202). Emerald Publishing Limited.

Jarek, K., & Mazurek, G. (2019). Marketing and artificial intelligence. *Central European Business Review, 8*(2), 46–55.

Jarrahi, M. H. (2018). Artificial intelligence and the future of work: Human-AI symbiosis in organizational decision making. *Business Horizons, 61*(4), 577–586. https://doi.org/10.1016/j.bushor.2018.03.007

Jebarajakirthy, C., Maseeh, H. I., Morshed, Z., Shankar, A., Arli, D., & Pentecost, R. (2021). Mobile advertising: A systematic literature review and future research agenda. *International Journal of Consumer Studies, 45*(6), 1258–1291.

Johnson, T., & Kaplan, R. S. (1987). *Relevance lost: The rise and fall of management accounting.* Harvard Business School Press.

Jurafsky, D., & Martin, J. H. (2018). Hidden Markov models. In *Speech and language processing* (3rd ed.). Stanford University. https://web.stanford.edu/~jurafsky/slp3

Kaplan, A., & Haenlein, M. (2019). Siri, Siri, in my hand: Who's the fairest in the land? On the interpretations, illustrations, and implications of artificial intelligence. *Business Horizons, 62*(1), 15–25. https://doi.org/10.1016/j.bushor.2018.08.004

Kaplan, A., & Haenlein, M. (2020). Rulers of the world, unite! The challenges and opportunities of artificial intelligence. *Business Horizons, 63*(1), 37–50.

Kaplan, J., et al. (2020). Scaling laws for neural language models. *arXiv preprint arXiv:2001.08361.* https://arxiv.org/abs/2001.08361

Kaput, M. (2024). *AI in advertising: Everything you need to know*. Marketing Artificial Intelligence Institute. https://www.marketingaiinstitute.com/blog/ai-in-advertising

Karttunen, L. (1974). Presupposition and linguistic context. *Theoretical Linguistics, 1*, 181–194. https://doi.org/10.1515/thli.1974.1.1-3.181

Kaur, K., Arumugam, N., Yunus, N. M. (2013). Beauty product advertisements: A critical discourse analysis. *Asian Social Science, 9*, 61–71. https://doi.org/10.5539/ass.v9n3p61

Ke, Q., & Wang, W. (2013). The adjective frequency in advertising English slogans. *Theory and Practice in Language Studies, 3*, 275–284. https://doi.org/10.4304/tpls.3.2.275-284

Keke, M. E. (2022). The use of digital marketing in information transport in social media: The example of Turkish companies. *Transportation Research Procedia, 63*, 2579–2588.

Khatun, A., & Brown, D. (2023). Reliability check: An analysis of GPT-3's response to sensitive topics and prompt wording. In *Proceedings of the 3rd Workshop on Trustworthy Natural Language Processing (TrustNLP 2023)*, (pp. 73–95), Toronto, Canada. Association for Computational Linguistics.

Khan, G. (2023). *Will AI-generated images create a new crisis for fact-checkers? Experts are not so sure*. Reuters Institute. https://reutersinstitute.politics.ox.ac.uk/news/will-ai-generated-images-create-new-crisis-fact-checkers-experts-are-not-so-sure

Koa, M. (2019). An analysis of language styles used in Revlon's written advertisements. *JELLT, 3*, 41–48. https://doi.org/10.36597/jellt.v3i1.4483

Kornberger, M., Pflueger, D., & Mouritsen, J. (2017). Evaluative infrastructures: Accounting for platform organization. *Accounting, Organizations and Society, 60*, 79–95.

Kövecses, Z. (2010). *Metaphor: A practical introduction*. Oxford University Press. ISBN: 0-19-514510-0

Kulp, P. (2023). ChatGPT upends advertising and marketing jobs. *Ad Week*. https://www.adweek.com/performance-marketing/chatgpt-is-already-influencing-skills-for-advertising-and-marketing-jobs/

Lahmann, M., Keiser, P., & Stierli, A. (2018). AI will transform project management. Are you ready? https://www.pwc.ch/en/insights/risk/transformation-assurance-ai-will-transform-project-management-are-you-ready.html

Lambert, C., Sponem S. (2012). Roles, authority and involvement of the management accounting function: A multiple case-study perspective, *European Accounting Review, 21(3)*, 565–589. https://doi.org/10.1080/09638180.2011.629415

Laux, J., Stephany, F., Russell, C., Wachter, S., & Mittelstadt, B. (2022). The Concentration-after-Personalisation Index (CAPI): Governing effects of personalisation using the example of targeted online advertising. *Big Data & Society, 9(2)*. https://doi.org/10.1177/20539517221132535

Lawton, G. (2023). *What is generative AI? Everything you need to know*. Tech Target. https://www.techtarget.com/searchenterpriseai/definition/generative-AI

Lee, C., Lee, G., & Lin, H. (2007). The role of organizational capabilities in successful e-business implementation. *Business Process Management Journal, 13(5)*, 677–693.

Lee, S. B. (2020). Chatbots and communication: The growing role of artificial intelligence in addressing and shaping customer needs. *Business Communication Research and Practice, 3*(2), 103–111. https://doi.org/10.22682/bcrp.2020.3.2.103

Lewiński, P. (1999). *Retoryka reklamy.* Wydawnictwo Uniwersytetu Wrocławskiego. ISBN: 83-229-1957-3

Lewis, M., & Dehler, G. (2000). Learning through Paradox: A Pedagogical strategy for exploring contradictions and complexity. *Journal of Management Education, 24,* 708–725. https//doi.org10.1177/105256290002400604

Li, C. (2020). OpenAI's GPT-3 language model: A technical overview. https://openai.com/research/gpt-3

Li, R., Kumar, A., & Chen, J. H. (2023). How chatbots and large language model artificial intelligence systems will reshape modern medicine: Fountain of creativity or Pandora's box? *JAMA Internal Medicine, 183,* 596–597.

Liebowitz, J. (2000). Knowledge management receptivity at a major pharmaceutical company. *Journal of Knowledge Management, 4*(3), 252–258. https://doi.org/10.1108/13673270010350057

Linghong, Z. (2006). The Linguistic Features of English Advertising. *CELEA Journal, 29,* 71–78.

Liu, Y., et al. (2023). Summary of ChatGPT/GPT-4 research and perspective towards the future of large language models. *arXiv:2304.01852 [cs].* https://arxiv.org/abs/2304.01852

Loten, A. (2023). Enterprise startups race to cash in on ChatGPT mania. *The Wall Street Journal.* https://www.wsj.com/articles/enterprise-startups-race-to-cash-in-on-chatgpt-mania-c04eeba

Ma, L., & Sun, B. (2020). Machine learning and AI in marketing – Connecting computing power to human insights. *International Journal of Research in Marketing, 37*(3), 481–504. https://doi.org/10.1016/j.ijresmar.2020.04.005

Malthouse, E., & Copulsky, J. (2023). Artificial intelligence ecosystems for marketing communications. *International Journal of Advertising, 42*(1), 128–140.

March, J. G. (1987). Ambiguity and accounting: The elusive link between information and decision making. *Accounting, Organizations and Society, 12(2),* 153–168.

Marcos, L., Babyn, P., & Alirezaie, J. (2024). Generative AI in medical imaging and its application in low dose computed tomography (CT) image denoising. In *Applications of generative AI.* Springer.

Mathew, J., & Scholar, P. G. (2021). A study into the use of artificial intelligence in e-commerce stock management and product suggestion generation for end users. In *Proceedings of the National Conference on Emerging Computer Applications (NCECA)* (p. 103).

Mick, D. G., & Fournier, S. (1998). Paradoxes of technology: Consumer cognizance, emotions, and coping strategies. *Journal of Consumer Research, 25*(2), 123–143.

Morales, J., & Lambert, C. (2013). Dirty work and the construction of identity. An ethnographic study of management accounting practices. *Accounting, Organizations and Society, 38(3),* 228–244.

Mounir, A. S. (2023). An overview of the functions and role of advertising as a communication tool in Belarus, Egypt, and the UK. *World Journal of Social Science Research, 10,* 29–40. https://doi.org/10.22158/wjssr.v10n2p29

Mühlhoff, R., & Willem, T. (2023). Social media advertising for clinical studies: Ethical and data protection implications of online targeting. *Big Data & Society, 10*(1), 1–15.

Muliyil, A. (2023, February 14). ChatGPT might just usher in the new era of renaissance for the advertising and media industry. *ET Brand Equity.* https://brandequity.economictimes.indiatimes.com/news/digital/chatgpt-might-just-usher-in-the-new-era-of-renaissance-for-the-advertising-and-media-industry/97887811

Munir, M. (2019). How artificial intelligence can help project managers. *Global Journal of Management and Business Research, 19*(1), 1–8.

Newmark, P. (1988). *A textbook of translation.* Prentice Hall.

Nezhad-Mokhtari, P., Javanbakht, S., Asadi, N., Ghorbani, M., Milani, M., Hanifehpour, Y., Gholizadeh, P., & Akbarzadeh, A. (2021). Recent advances in honey-based hydrogels for wound healing applications: Towards natural therapeutics. *Journal of Drug Delivery Science and Technology, 66.*

Nickerson, J. A., & Zenger, T. R. (2004). A knowledge-based theory of the firm—The problem-solving perspective. *Organization Science, 15*(6), 617–632.

Nicolescu, L., & Tudorache, M. T. (2022). Human-computer interaction in customer service: The experience with AI chatbots—a systematic literature review. *Electronics, 11*(10), 1579. https://doi.org/10.3390/electronics11101579

Nikolajeva, A., & Teilans, A. (2021). Machine learning technology overview in terms of digital marketing and personalization. In L. Campanile & A. Bargiela (Eds.), *ECMS* (pp. 125–130). European Council for Modelling and Simulation (ECMS).

Noponen, N. (2019). Impact of artificial intelligence on management. *Electronic Journal of Business Ethics and Organization Studies, 24*(1), 43–50.

Nov, O., Singh, N., & Mann, D. M. (2023). Putting ChatGPT's medical advice to the (Turing) test. *medRxiv.* https://www.medrxiv.org/content/10.1101/2023.02.20.23286157v1

Nowacki, R. (2006). *Reklama.* Difin SA. ISBN: 978-83-7251-542-1

Oppenlaender, J. (2022). The creativity of text-to-image generation. In *Proceedings of the 25th International Academic Mindtrek Conference (Academic Mindtrek '22)* (pp. 192–202). ACM. https://doi.org/10.1145/3569219.3569352

Osadchaya, E., Marder, B., Yule, J. A., Yau, A., Lavertu, L., Stylos, N., & AlRabiah, S. (2024). To ChatGPT, or not to ChatGPT: Navigating the paradoxes of generative AI in the advertising industry. *Business Horizons.*

Ouyang, L., et al. (2022). Training language models to follow instructions with human feedback. https://arxiv.org/abs/2203.02155

Ozbayoglu, A. M., Gudelek, M. U., & Sezer, O. B. (2020). Deep learning for financial applications: A survey. *Applied Soft Computing, 93*, 106384.

Patel, D., & Wong, G. (2023). GPT-4 architecture, infrastructure, training dataset, costs, vision, MoE. https://www.gpt-4.info

Pedersen, C. L. (2023). The paradoxical marketer: Interpretations, illustrations, and implications. *Business Horizons, 66*(6), 765–784.

Pérez-Sobrino, P. (2013). Metaphor use in advertising: Analysis of the interaction between multimodal metaphor and metonymy in a greenwashing advertisement. In E. Gola & F. Ervas (Eds.), *Metaphor in focus: philosophical perspectives on metaphor use* (pp. 67–82). Cambridge Scholars Publishing.

Perloff, R. M. (2017). *The dynamics of persuasion: Communication and attitudes in the 21st century.* Taylor & Francis. ISBN: 978-1-138-10032-9

Peter, C., Verhoef, P. K., Kannan, J., Jeffrey, I. (2015). From multi-channel retailing to omni-channel retailing: Introduction to the special issue on multi-channel retailing. *Journal of Retailing, 91(2)*, 174–181.

Petrescu, M., & Krishen, A. S. (2023). Hybrid intelligence: Human–AI collaboration in marketing analytics. *Journal of Marketing Analytics, 11*(3), 263–274. https://doi.org/10.1057/s41270-023-00245-3

Prelipceanu, C. (2013). Advertising and language manipulation. *Diversité et identité culturelle en Europe, 10*, 247–254.

Qi, G., & Zhu, Z. (2021). Blockchain and Artificial Intelligence applications. *Journal of Artificial Intelligence and Technology, 1(2)*, 83. https://doi.org/10.37965/jait.2021.0019

Quattrone, P. (2016). Management accounting goes digital: Will the move make it wiser? *Management Accounting Research, 31*, 118–122.

Radford, A., & Narasimhan, K. (2018). Improving language understanding by generative pre-training. https://openai.com/research/language-understanding

Radford, A., Wu, J., Child, R., Luan, D., Amodei, D., & Sutskever, I. (2019). Language models are unsupervised multitask learners. https://openai.com/research/language-understanding

Raisch, S., & Krakowski, S. (2020). Artificial intelligence and management: The automation-augmentation paradox. *Academy of Management Review.* https://doi.org/10.5465/amr.2018.0072

Raiter, O. (2021). Segmentation of bank consumers for Artificial Intelligence marketing. *International Journal of Contemporary Financial Issues, 1(1)*, 39–54.

Rasakumaran, A. (2018). Euphemism as a persuasive advertising strategy. *Journal of Business Management, 1*, 22–33.

Ray, N. M., Ryder M. E., Scott S. V. (1991). Toward an understanding of the Use of Foreign Words in Print Advertising. *Journal of International Consumer Marketing, 3*, 69–98. https://doi.org/10.1300/J046v03n04_06

Ray, P., Torck, A., Quigley, L., Wangzhou, A., Neiman, M., Rao, C., Lam, T., Kim, J. Y., Kim, T. H., Zhang, M. Q., Dussor, G., & Price, T. J. (2018). Comparative transcriptome profiling of the human and mouse dorsal root ganglia: An RNA-seq-based resource for pain and sensory neuroscience research. *Pain, 159(7)*, 1325–1345. doi: 10.1097/j.pain.0000000000001217

Revell, G. (2024). Generative AI applications in the health and well-being domain: Virtual and robotic assistance and the need for niche language models (NLMs). In *Applications of generative AI*. Springer.

Rialti, R., Filieri, R., Zollo, L., Bazi, S., & Ciappei, C. (2022). Assessing the relationship between gamified advertising and in-app purchases: A consumers' benefits-based perspective. *International Journal of Advertising, 41(5)*, 868–891.

Richards, J. I., & Curran, C. M. (2002). Oracles on "advertising": Searching for a definition. *Journal of Advertising, 31*, 63–77. https://doi.org/10.1080/00913367.2002.10673667

Romanik, A. (2014). Przymiotniki wartościujące w reklamie (na materiale rosyjskiej prasy kobiecej). *Acta Neophilologica, 1*, 107–114.

Romanova I. D., & Smirnova I. V. (2019). Persuasive techniques in advertising. *Training, Language and Culture, 3*, 55–70. https://doi.org/10.29366/2019tlc.3.2.4

Roumeliotis, K. I., & Tselikas, N. D. (2023). ChatGPT and open-AI models: A preliminary review. *Future Internet, 15*(192). https://doi.org/10.3390/fi15060192

Rush, S. (1998). The noun phrase in advertising English. *Journal of Pragmatics, 29*, 155–171. https://doi.org/10.1016/S0378-2166(97)00053-2

Salloum, S. A., Al-Emran, M., & Shaalan, K. (2018). The impact of knowledge sharing on information systems: A review. In L. Uden, B. Hadzima, & I.-H. Ting (Eds.), *International Conference on knowledge management in organizations* (pp. 94–102). Springer.

Sanzogni, L., Guzman, G., & Busch, P. (2017). Artificial intelligence and knowledge management: Questioning the tacit dimension. *Prometheus, 35*(1), 37–56. https://doi.org/10.1080/08109028.2017.136454

Schildt, H. (2017). Big data and organizational design: The brave new world of algorithmic management and computer augmented transparency. *Innovation, 19(1)*, 23–30.

Şenyapar, H. N. (2024). The future of marketing: The transformative power of artificial intelligence. *International Journal of Management and Administration, 8*(15), 1–19. https://doi.org/10.29064/ijma.1412272

Shariq, M. (2020). Tools & techniques used in the language of advertisements: A linguistic analysis of Indian TV commercial ads. *Media Watch, 11*, 564–578. https://doi.org/10.15655/mw/2020/11092020

Shawar, B. & Atwell, E. (2007). Chatbots: Are they really useful? *LDV Forum, 22*, 29–49.

Sintonen, T., & Auvinen, T. (2009). Who is leading, leader or story? *Tamara Journal or Critical Organization Inquiry, 8(2)*.

Sirkka, L. J., & Lang, K. R. (2005). Managing the paradoxes of mobile technology. *Information Systems Management, 22*(4), 7–23.

Skubis, I. (2020). *Pluricentryzm języka niemieckiego w języku prawa karnego Niemiec, Austrii i Szwajcarii*. Wydawnictwo Adam Marszałek. ISBN: 978-83-8180-374-8

Skubis, I. (2021). Językoznawstwo jako bezpieczna dyscyplina dla badań nad sztuczną inteligencją. In B. Fischer, A. Pązik, & M. Świerczyński (Eds.), *Prawo sztucznej inteligencji i nowych technologii* (pp. 169–181). Wolters Kluwer.

Skubis, I. (2022a). Pluricentrism in education and communication – Lexical differences in English and German varieties – Outcomes of the research. In *Kultura i Edukacja* (pp. 143–164).

Skubis, I. (2022b). The importance of co-teaching in teaching German varieties. In B. Pituła & M. Kowalski (Eds.), *Co-teaching – Everyday life or terra incognita of contemporary education?* (pp. 223–236). Vandenhoeck & Ruprecht Verlag.

Skubis, I. (2024). *Ética, terminología, opiniones y el mercado de SexTech: un análisis multidisciplinario sobre los robots sexuales*. Wydawnictwo Politechniki Śląskiej. ISBN: 978-83-7880-957-9

Skubis, I. (2024). Seksroboty – Zarządzanie Etyką i Zarządzanie Innowacjami w Branży Sextech. In *Management and quality* [in print].

Skubis, I., & Akahome, J. (2022). Exploring transformational customer experience in digital banking: An exploratory study. *Organization & Management Scientific Quarterly, 3*, 97–112. https://doi.org/10.29119/1899-6116.2022.59.7

Skubis, I., & Damas, K. (2024). Language of advertising on the example of selected hair products advertisements. *Scientific Papers of Silesian University of Technology*. In press.

Skubis, I., & Mosek, M. (2024). Language of advertising in the tourism industry. *Scientific Papers of Silesian University of Technology*. In press.

Skubis, I., & Wodarski, K. (2023). Humanoid robots in managerial positions – Decision-making process and human oversight. *Scientific Papers of Silesian University of Technology, 189*, 573–596. https://doi.org/10.29119/1641-3466.2023.189.36

Skubis, I., Wodarski, K., Boch, A. (2023). Language in the human-technology era. New terminology on the sex (robot) market –"digisexuality", "technosexuality" and "robosexuality" – a multilingual analysis and survey among students. *Scientific Papers of Silesian University of Technology, 189*, 553–572. http://dx.doi.org/10.29119/1641-3466.2023.189.35

Sloane, T. O. (2006). *Encyclopedia of rhetoric*. Oxford University Press. ISBN: 978-0195125955

Smith, K. (2004). 'I am me, but who are you and what are we?': The translation of personal pronouns and possessive determiners in advertising texts. *Multilingua - Journal of Cross-Cultural and Interlanguage Communication, 23*, 283–303. https://doi.org/10.1515/mult.2004.013

Sokół, A. (2008). Perswazja czy manipulacja? Analiza wybranych aspektów językowych czasopisma Wróżka. *Zborník príspevkov z XVIII. kolokvia mladých jazykovedcov*, 644–660.

Somasundaram, M., Junaid, K. M., & Mangadu, S. (2020). Artificial Intelligence (AI) enabled Intelligent Quality Management System (IQMS) for personalized learning path. *Procedia Computer Science, 172*, 438–442. https://doi.org/10.1016/j.procs.2020.05.096

Sundström, A. (2024). AI in management control: Emergent forms, practices, and infrastructures. *Critical Perspectives on Accounting, 99*, 102701. https://doi.org/10.1016/j.cpa.2023.102701

Susnjak, T., & McIntosh, T. R. (2024). ChatGPT: The end of online exam integrity? *Education Sciences, 14*(6), 656. https://doi.org/10.3390/educsci14060656

Sutherland, J., Belec, J., Sheikh, A., Chepelev, L., Althobaity, W., Chow, B. J., & La Russa, D. J. (2019). Applying modern virtual and augmented reality technologies to medical images and models. *Journal of Digital Imaging, 32*, 38–53.

Szczęsna, E. (2001). *Poetyka reklamy*. Wydawnictwo Naukowe PWN S.A. ISBN: 83-01-13538-7

Taherdoost, H., & Madanchian, M. (2023). Artificial intelligence and knowledge management: Impacts, benefits, and implementation. *Computers, 12*(4), 72. https://doi.org/10.3390/computers12040072

Taiwo, R., et al. (2024). Generative AI in the construction industry: A state-of-the-art analysis. https://arxiv.org/abs/2402.09939

Teodorescu, A. (2015). Linguistic patterns in advertising messages. *Knowledge Horizons – Economics, 7*, 115–118.

Tokarz, M. (2002). Argumentacja i perswazja. *Filozofia Nauki, 3*, 5–39.

Torto, R. T. (2016). An analysis of descriptive features in the English used in an advertising text. *International Journal of Linguistics and Communication, 4*, 47–55. https://doi.org/10.15640/ijlc.v4n2a4

Tristanto, T. A., Hurriyati, R., Dirgantari, P. D., & Elyusufi, A. M. (2021). AIDA model as a marketing strategy to influence consumer buying interest in the digital age. *Budapest International Research and Critics Institute-Journal, 4*, 12575–12586. https://doi.org/10.33258/birci.v4i4.3319

Tu, R., Ma, C., & Zhang, C. (2023). Causal-discovery performance of ChatGPT in the context of neuropathic pain diagnosis. https://arxiv.org/abs/2301.13819

van Zelst, S. J.; van Dongen, B. F.; van der Aalst, W. M. (2018). Event stream-based process discovery using abstract representations. *Knowl. Inf. Syst, 54*, 407–435.

Vaswani, A., et al. (2017). Attention is all you need. https://arxiv.org/abs/1706.03762

Verma, S., Sharma, R., Deb, S., & Maitra, D. (2021). Artificial intelligence in marketing: Systematic review and future research direction. *International Journal of Information Management Data Insights, 1*(1), 100002.

Vlačić, B., Corbo, L., Costa e Silva, S., & Dabić, M. (2021). The evolving role of artificial intelligence in marketing: A review and research agenda. *Journal of Business Research, 128*, 187–203. https://doi.org/10.1016/j.jbusres.2021.01.055

Wahde, M., & Virgolin, M. (2022). Conversational agents: Theory and applications. *arXiv.* https://arxiv.org/abs/2202.03164

Wales, K. (2011). *A dictionary of stylistics.* Taylor & Francis. ISBN: 978-1-4082-3115-9

Wang, W., & Siau, K. (2022). Artificial Intelligence, machine learning, automation, robotics, future of work and future of humanity. In Management Association (Ed.), *Research Anthology on Machine Learning Techniques, Methods, and Applications* (pp. 1460–1481). IGI Global. https://doi.org/10.4018/978-1-6684-6291-1.ch076

Westphal, E., & Seitz, H. (2024). Generative artificial intelligence: Analyzing its future applications in additive manufacturing. *Big Data and Cognitive Computing, 8*(74). https://doi.org/10.3390/bdcc8070074

White, J., Fu, Q., Hays, S., Sandborn, M., Olea, C., Gilbert, H., Elnashar, A., Spencer-Smith, J., & Schmidt, D. C. (2023). A prompt pattern catalog to enhance prompt engineering with ChatGPT. *arXiv preprint arXiv:2302.11382.* https://arxiv.org/abs/2302.11382

Wiktor, J. (2011). Komunikacja marketingowa - perswazja czy manipulacja? W stronę reguły 30–70. *Zeszyty Naukowe / Uniwersytet Ekonomiczny w Poznaniu, 208,* 11–22.

Wilson, H. J., & Daugherty, P. R. (2018). Collaborative intelligence: Humans and AI are joining forces. *Harvard Business Review, 96*(4), 114–123.

Wiredu, J. (2023). An investigation on the characteristics, abilities, constraints, and functions of Atificial Intelligence (AI): The age of ChatGPT as an essential. *Information and Management, 108*(3), 62614–62620.

Wołk, A., Skowrońska, H., & Skubis, I. (2021). Multilingual chatbot for e-commerce: Data generation and machine translation. *PACIS 2021 Proceedings, 232,* 1–14.

Wołk, K., Wołk, A., Wnuk, D., & Grześ, T., & Skubis, I. (2022). Survey on dialogue systems including Slavic languages. *Neurocomputing, 2022,* 62–84.

Wu, L., & Hu, Y.-P. (2018). Open innovation based knowledge management implementation: A mediating role of knowledge management design. *Journal of Knowledge Management, 22*(8), 1736–1756. https://doi.org/10.1108/JKM-06-2016-0238

Xia, C., Zhang, A., Wang, H., Zhang, B., & Zhang, Y. (2023). Bidirectional urban flows in rapidly urbanizing metropolitan areas and their macro and micro impacts on urban growth: A case study of the Yangtze River middle reaches megalopolis. *China. Land Use Policy, 82,* 158–168.

Yam, K. C., Goh, E.-Y., Fehr, R., Lee, R., Soh, H., & Gray, K. (2022). When your boss is a robot: Workers are more spiteful to robot supervisors that seem more human. *Journal of Experimental Social Psychology, 102,* 1–12. https://doi.org/10.1016/j.jesp.2022.104360

Yang, X., Li, H., Ni, L., & Li, T. (2021). Application of artificial intelligence in precision marketing. *Journal of Organizational and End User Computing, 33*(4), 209–219.

Yano, K. (2017). How artificial intelligence will change HR. *People Strategy, 40*(1), 42–47.

Yau, K.-L. A., Saad, N. M., & Chong, Y.-W. (2021). Artificial Intelligence Marketing (AIM) for enhancing customer relationships. *Applied Sciences, 11*(18), Article 18. https://doi.org/10.3390/app11188562

Yeğin, T. (2020). The place and future of artificial intelligence in marketing strategies. *EKEV Akademi Dergisi, 81,* Article 81.

Young, S. C. (2017). *Brilliant Persuasion: Everyday techniques to boost your powers of persuasion.* Pearson Education Limited. ISBN: 978-1-292-13573-1

Zawacki-Richter, O., Marín, V. I., Bond, M., & Gouverneur, F. (2019). Systematic review of research on artificial intelligence applications in higher education—where are the educators? *International Journal of Educational Technology in Higher Education, 16*(1), 39.

Zhang, C., Zhang, C., Zheng, S., Qiao, Y., Li, C., Zhang, M., Dam, S. K., Thwal, C. M., Tun, Y. L., Huy, L. L., Kim, D., Bae, S.-H., Lee, L.-H., Yang, Y., Shen, H. T., Kweon, I. S., & Hong, C. S. (2023). A complete survey on generative AI (AIGC): Is ChatGPT from GPT-4 to GPT-5 all you need? *arXiv preprint.* arXiv:2303.11717.

Zhang, Q., Lu, J., & Jin, Y. (2021). Artificial intelligence in recommender systems. *Complex & Intelligent Systems, 7,* 439–457.

Zhang, X., Wang, Y., & Lv, P. (2017). *IBBAS: A visual analytics system of large-scale traffic data for bus body advertising.* 18th International Conference on Parallel and Distributed Computing, Applications and Technologies (PDCAT) (pp. 67–74). IEEE.

Zhang, Y., & Gosline, R. (2023). Human favoritism, not AI aversion: People's perceptions (and bias) toward generative AI, human experts, and human–GAI collaboration in persuasive content generation. *Judgment and Decision Making, e41.* https://doi.org/10.1017/jdm.2023.37

Zhou, C., Qiu, C., & Acuna, D. E. (2022). Paraphrase identification with deep learning: A review of datasets and methods. *arXiv preprint arXiv:2212.06933.* https://arxiv.org/abs/2212.06933

Zhuo, T. Y., Huang, Y., Chen, C., & Xing, Z. (2023). Exploring AI ethics of ChatGPT: A diagnostic analysis. *arXiv preprint arXiv:2301.12867.* https://arxiv.org/abs/2301.12867

NETOGRAPHY

Adriel Blog. *The Future of Advertising Is Here: How AI is Reshaping the Industry.* Retrieved July 18, 2024, from https://www.adriel.com/blog/the-future-of-advertising-is-ai

American Marketing Association. *Definition of Advertising.* Retrieved July 12, 2024, from https://marketing-dictionary.org/a/advertising/

Cambridge Dictionary. *Imperative sentence.* Retrieved May 4, 2022, from https://dictionary.cambridge.org/dictionary/english/imperative-sentence

Cambridge Dictionary. *Interrogative Sentence.* Retrieved May 4, 2022, from https://dictionary.cambridge.org/dictionary/english/interrogative-sentence

Chuandao, Y. (2005). *Rhetorical Characteristics of Advertising English.* Retrieved May 28, 2022, from http://languageinindia.com/march2005/advertisingenglishhongkong2.html

Collins English Dictionary. *Linger.* Retrieved July 22, 2024, from https://www.collinsdictionary.com/dictionary/english/linger

Collins English Dictionary. *Metaphor.* Retrieved July 8, 2024, from https://www.collinsdictionary.com/dictionary/english/metaphor

Collins English Dictionary. *Personal Pronoun.* Retrieved May 4, 2022, from https://www.collinsdictionary.com/dictionary/english/personal-pronoun

Collins English Dictionary. *Soiree.* Retrieved July 22, 2024, from https://www.collinsdictionary.com/dictionary/english/soiree

Collins English Dictionary. *To Speak Volumes.* Retrieved July 22, 2024, from https://www.collinsdictionary.com/dictionary/english/to-speak-volumes

Comas, J. (2003). *"Rhetoric" – An Etymology of the Greek Word from Homer to Plato.* Retrieved July 8, 2024, from https://capone.mtsu.edu/jcomas/rhetoric/etymology.html

Deepmind Google. Retrieved July 18, 2024, from https://deepmind.google

Eidenmuller, M. E. (2001). *Scholarly Definitions of Rhetoric.* Retrieved July 8, 2024, from https://www.americanrhetoric.com/rhetoricdefinitions.htm

Farlex Dictionary of Idioms. (2015). *A feast for the eyes.* Retrieved June 14, 2022, from https://idioms.thefreedictionary.com/a+feast+for+the+eyes

Google Blog. Retrieved July 18, 2023, from https://blog.google

Harper, D. (2020). *Etymology of Advertisement.* Online Etymology Dictionary. Retrieved June 17, 2024, from https://www.etymonline.com/word/advertisement

Harper, D. *Etymology of Advertise.* Online Etymology Dictionary. Retrieved January 29, 2022, from https://www.etymonline.com/word/advertise

Harper, D. *Etymology of Euphemism.* Online Etymology Dictionary. Retrieved June 7, 2022, from https://www.etymonline.com/word/euphemism#etymonline_v_11682

Harper, D. *Etymology of Hyperbole.* Online Etymology Dictionary. Retrieved May 28, 2022, from https://www.etymonline.com/word/hyperbole

Harper, D. *Etymology of Metaphor.* Online Etymology Dictionary. Retrieved May 28, 2022, from https://www.etymonline.com/word/metaphor

Lexico Dictionary. *Euphemism*. Retrieved June 7, 2022, from https://www.lexico.com/definition/euphemism

Longman Dictionary of Contemporary English. *Advertisement*. Retrieved January 29, 2022, from https://www.ldoceonline.com/dictionary/advertisement

Merriam-Webster. *Advertisement*. Merriam-Webster.com dictionary. Retrieved January 29, 2022, from https://www.merriam-webster.com/dictionary/advertisement

Merriam-Webster. *Antidote*. Merriam-Webster.com dictionary. Retrieved June 14, 2022, from https://www.merriam-webster.com/thesaurus/antidote

Merriam-Webster. *Hangry*. Merriam-Webster.com dictionary. Retrieved June 14, 2022, from https://www.merriam-webster.com/dictionary/hangry

Merriam-Webster. *Manipulate*. Merriam-Webster.com dictionary. Retrieved June 6, 2022, from https://www.merriam-webster.com/dictionary/manipulate

Merriam-Webster. *Metaphor*. Merriam-Webster.com dictionary. Retrieved May 28, 2022, from https://www.merriam-webster.com/dictionary/metaphor

Merriam-Webster. *Minor sentence*. Merriam-Webster.com dictionary. Retrieved May 5, 2022, from https://www.merriam-webster.com/dictionary/minor%20sentence

Merriam-Webster. *Persuade*. Merriam-Webster.com dictionary. Retrieved January 30, 2022, from https://www.merriam-webster.com/dictionary/persuade

Merriam-Webster. *Simile*. Merriam-Webster.com dictionary. Retrieved June 7, 2022, from https://www.merriam-webster.com/dictionary/simile#note-1

Merriam-Webster. *Weasel Word*. Merriam-Webster.com dictionary. Retrieved June 6, 2022, from https://www.merriam-webster.com/dictionary/weasel%20word

Microsoft Bing. *Overview of Microsoft Search in Bing*. Retrieved July 18, 2024 from https://learn.microsoft.com/en-us/microsoftsearch/overview-microsoft-search-bing

Mitchell, K. *Alliteration Effects*. Retrieved May 28, 2022, from http://msmitchellsclasses.weebly.com/uploads/4/6/7/4/4674576/alliteration_chart.pdf

Open AI. *Best Practices for Prompt Engineering with the OpenAI API*. Retrieved July 18, 2024, from https://help.openai.com/en/articles/6654000-best-practices-for-prompt-engineering-with-openai-api

Open AI. Retrieved July 18, 2024, from https://openai.com

The AI Agency. *AI in Advertising: Pros, Cons, Tools, Use Cases, and Everything You Need to Know*. Retrieved July 18, 2024, from https://theaiagency.io/ai-marketing/ai-advertising/

Vasiloaia, M. (2018). *Linguistic Features of the Language of Advertising*. Retrieved January 30, 2022, from https://www.ugb.ro/etc/etc2009no1/s0804%20(2).pdf

Wordstream Blog. *7 AI Marketing Trends for 2024 & What They Mean for You*. Retrieved July 16, 2024, from https://www.wordstream.com/blog/ai-marketing-trends-2024

Index

Printed in the United States
by Baker & Taylor Publisher Services